Journey Of
Struggle,
Journey In Hope

Journey Of Struggle, Journey In Hope

Jane Heaton

People and Their Pilgrimage in "Central Africa"

Friendship Press, New York

Library of Congress Cataloging in Publication Data

Heaton, Jane
　　Journey of Struggle, Journey of Hope.

1. Christianity — Africa, Central — addresses, essays, lectures.　2. Africa, Central — church history — addresses, essays, lectures.　I. Heaton, Jane, 1931 -

BR1430.J68 1983　　　　　　　　276.7'082　　　　　　　　82-24187
ISBN 0-377-00126-0

ISBN 0-377-00126-0

Editorial Office: 475 Riverside Drive, Room 772, New York, NY 10115
Distribution Office: P.O. Box 37844, Cincinnati, OH 45237

Dedicated To:

The 53 women who attended the Pan-African Leadership Course for Women from 1975-1977 and the staff of the Women's Training Center, Mindolo Ecumenical Foundation, Kitwe, Zambia. They gave me a deep appreciation and knowledge of African life and culture and they allowed me to become a part of their lives for a few years.

Contents

Introduction

After more than 400 years of contact, Africa remains in the minds of many people in the western world a "Dark Continent" inhabited with primitive people and wild animals, covered with thick jungle, and ruled by the "noble savage." Even today, in the last decades of the 20th century, for many people Africa remains the Africa of Tarzan.

Ironically, the closer the West gets to Africa, the "darker" Africa becomes. To many, Africa remains a land teeming with pagans and Muslims who need to be converted by western missionaries to Christianity.

Others see Africa as nothing but a land bleeding with poverty, hunger, disease, malnutrition, war, disaster, and all kinds of political, social, and economic instabilities. For some, Africa does not exist except when there is an earthquake, famine, flood, tornado or a coup d'etat.

To these people, Africa has nothing to give, but everything to receive. Africa, indeed, has become for them an object of pity and therefore an object of other people's salvation. But this is not accurate.

Any sincere study of Africa past and present will reveal how much Africa offers the world community.

—Africa is the second largest continent in the world and covers about 20 percent of the earth's surface. About 10 percent of the world's people live in Africa.

—Africa has large amounts of arable agricultural land and produces mainly export products such as cocoa, coffee, palm, cotton, rubber, sisal and tea.

—Africa has the largest desert in the world, the Sahara, and some of the world's largest and most useful rivers.

—Algeria, Angola, Libya, Tunisia, Egypt, Morocco, Nigeria, Gabon and Congo Republic, all in Africa, are among the world's leading natural gas and petroleum producing countries.

—Africa is considered the richest continent in the world because of large shares of the world's mineral resources including chromium, diamond, cobalt, gold, phosphate, platinum and others.

—Leading anthropologists claim Africa is the home of all humankind because the first human species was found in East Africa near Lake Turkana. Africa was the cradle of the world's civilization along the banks of the Tigris and Euphrates Rivers.

—Africa is the most polyglot continent in the world, with about 800 to 1,000 different, separate and distinct languages. Yet Africa is cursed to use, officially, three foreign languages— English, French and Portuguese.

—Africa is the continent that gave refuge to Jesus when King Herod wanted to kill him. Today, Africa has over five million refugees; estimates are that one in every 100 people in Africa is a refugee. They represent about one-third of the world's refugee population of 16 million or more.

Disturbing questions spring to mind at this point. How can a continent with such wealth and potential be considered poor, destitute, hungry and unstable? People hunger in a land of plenty. Why? What happened in Africa's history to bring Africa to this place?

A SHORT HISTORY

The present social, economic and political predicaments in Africa are rooted to a large extent in colonialism watered by neocolonialism.

In 1884-85, during the colonial period, Britain, France, Belgium and Portugal divided up Africa with no regard for racial, linguistic, ethnic and religious groups. These artificially imposed boundaries disrupted extended family and community ties thus destroying cohesive African societies. These colonial frontiers were, and indeed still are, at odds with Africa's natural loyalties to ethnic communities, peoples and families. The African communal spirit is killed, and buried, by these outside methods of divide and rule.

The current period of neocolonialism includes participation in African economic and political affairs by Canada and the United States, nations that were once colonies. Neocolonialism is especially marked by the activities of multinational corporations.

TIME BOMBS

The economic time bomb has its roots undoubtedly in this colonialism and neocolonialism. During the colonial era, most African countries were forced to begin producing cash crops in order to pay taxes to their colonial rulers. They eventually came to produce single cash crops, using their arable land for the production of crops for export. For example, Ghana, the leading cocoa producing country in the world grows about 55 percent of the world's supply of cocoa. Kenya is famous for tea; Uganda, for coffee; and Tanzania, for sisal and cashew nuts.

Modern African governments have been forced to use their rich resources of labor, land and capital in growing export crops to meet the payments of their trade deficits. These crops go to feed already over fed westerners while Africans suffer the agonies of hunger and malnutrition. Farmers with small land holdings who once produced food for their own consumption are constantly encouraged, and sometimes coerced, to produce crops for export. The farmers become poor. The economic time bomb becomes a poverty time bomb.

African countries usually have little or no say in the prices of their products. They are in fact "price-takers" and not "price-makers." Due to the blatant exploitation of the masses by western countries, in collusion with the African elite, most hard working persons come out empty-handed, at best.

Another part of this injustice is that Africa was made, and still is, a huge market for western-made industrialized products. Since the western countries are usually price-makers they can charge exorbitant prices for their manufactured goods. For instance, a Ugandan farmer would have to sell at least 400 tons of coffee in order to be able to buy one tractor. The unfair world trade system has lead many African countries into a heavy trade deficit and huge international debts.

Tourism has now become another strong arm of pollution and exploitation of African arts, cultural and value systems. Tourists have taken over areas which were once used by Africans and have turned items of creative and spiritual value, such as rituals, ceremonies and art, into objects of monetary value.

Africa is constantly referred to as poor, hungry and malnourished. Africa, as a matter of fact, is not poor in itself. Africa has been impoverished, dispossessed, disinherited, raped and robbed of dignity and integrity.

THE FUTURE

Africa is full of hope and ready to pick up the challenge to recover lost identity and wealth. Africa's cultural and religious verve are the two strong pillars on which the future lies. About 55 percent of Africa's population is youth. Africa still has large areas of arable land. The young nations in Africa have the potential to change.

The African communal philosophy says, "I am because we are, and because we are, I am." Portraying the concept of sharing, the African philosophy insists more on participation than achievement. Achievement may be vertical, but consumption is always horizontal. The value of individuals does not lie in how much they have in the bank, but their worth as human beings made in the image of God.

African cultures hold that anything taken from nature must be paid back 10 times. Africans revere nature and therefore do not expect anything good from nature if nature is treated badly. This ethic is one of learning to live with nature rather than one of conquering nature. The African, in this respect, sees that the whole cosmos is a religious and spiritual arena, with spirits interacting with the human for good or bad.

Africans have quite rightly been described as incurably religious. Religion plays a major role in everything the African does. There are three main religions in Africa. Traditional African religion is often not easily distinguished from cultural, social and daily life. A strong belief exists in nature and the cosmos as a religious phenomenon and a living reality. The African's dependence on and respect for nature gives credence to the full range of life's activities and philosophies.

Islam and Christianity are the other two religions; both are basically missionary religions. Christianity through the work of evangelization by word and deed opened up Africa to the rest of the world. The missionaries built schools, hospitals, and participated in other development programs. In fact, the church spearheaded the struggle for independence and liberation of Africa. By translating the Bible into many African languages the church enabled many African converts to demand the tenants of the Gospel commands from their colonial rulers and other oppressors.

The church has found Africa a fertile soil for growth and development. The church has come to live in Africa. African Christians and theologians are trying daily to root the church in Africa and get rid of its foreign wrappings. Africans through their own efforts want to see a church marked: "MADE IN AFRICA!" They want to be able to answer the question Jesus is asking African Christians daily, "Who do you African Christians say that I am?" Africans through their own experiences are able to tell the world who Jesus Christ is.

An estimated 100 million black Africans are Christians. Some say the number is much higher. Researchers further say that Africa is the continent where Christianity is growing at the fastest pace, a rate of six percent per year. With this rate of growth, it is estimated that by the turn of the century, Africa will be the most Christian continent in the world with an estimated 150 million Christians.

This present work on the people and their pilgrimage in "Central Africa," stretching from the Sahara south to the Zambezi River, is an attempt to correct the image of Africa as needing instead of Africa as giving. The term "Central Africa" as it is used in this work does not correspond directly to the traditional geographical, cultural and economic or political division of Africa. The emphasis here is to share the potentials, challenges, needs, hopes, and aspirations of these African countries in that area of the continent. Whenever it was found necessary, references were also made to the entire continent, since more than anything Africans want to stress the unity of the continent.

This book on "Central Africa" therefore, comes as a telescopic attempt, or a bird's eye view, if only to whet your appetite to learn and know more about this giant, rich, turbulent, but hopeful part of the world.

It is hoped that it will help correct some of the misconceptions, stereotypes and ignorance exhibited through the television screens and media of the western world. This book should help to shake the cobwebs from the eyes of the sincere seeker and the skeptic alike.

Africa is still at a crossroad. Africa remains a question mark, "Which way Africa?" But sons and daughters of Africa are still hopeful that, as the scripture promises, "Ethiopia shall arise."

—**Kofi Appiah-Kubi,** author of
Man Cures/God Heals

Preface

Purpose: To help the reader share and understand some of the joys, celebrations, pains and struggles experienced by the people of "Central Africa."

Format: *Reader's Digest* size and format. Book will contain articles of varying subjects and lengths.

Countries to be included: Sao Tome and Principe, Sierra Leone, Equitorial Guinea, Togo, Cameroun, Ivory Coast, Nigeria, Zaire, Benin, Ghana, Burundi, Uganda, Kenya, Tanzania, Seychelles, Sudan, Ethiopia, Somalia, Malawi, Zambia, Liberia, Rwanda, Gabon, Congo, Djibouti and the Central African Republic.

The articles in this book, assembled from various magazines and books and from various writers, were chosen to give a multi-faceted picture of life in African countries from coast-to-coast, South of the Sahara and North of the Zambezi River. Many of the articles are of a general nature. Some of the material details problem situations in only one country. However, the majority of the countries included in this study experience similar problems and joys. The choice of articles, because of the vast amount of information and material, was difficult.

In 1977, after spending almost three years teaching in Kitwe, Zambia, I traveled through 14 African countries visiting former students and contacting church and community leaders about training possibilities for their personnel. In every country I was impressed with the development taking place and the response of people to opportunities for education and training. Students competed for limited places in schools. More than 90 women registered for a four-month rural craft course with only two staff members. Agricultural schools have to turn away students because of lack of housing facilities. Twenty-four students are willing to crowd into a classroom built for 15 in order to take a five-month leadership training course. Fish traps and baskets are made by men and women in a rural village as a source of income. Refugees study how to become teachers of teachers, looking forward to the time they return to their own country. On and on the list goes.

Most of all I was impressed by the people I met—from squatter communities to state houses. Their major concern is how to provide adequate shelter, food, clothing and education for their families. It is hoped that this study will help you understand the struggles of the people of "Central Africa" in their day-to-day living and to understand the place of the church in that struggle.

Identity is important to all of us and we all must be free to establish that identity. So that, too, is what this book is about—a search to understand the identity of African Christianity, an African theology, African music and African worship. We may not like what some of the authors say about western domination in church and community life. But we can read and study with an open mind and heart. We can try to understand what it is like to live with someone else's set of values and customs. Then, from a new perspective, learn how we can walk and work hand-in-hand with African Christians.

This book could not have been compiled without the help of many, many persons, especially the members of the Commission on Education for Mission Task Force on Africa, who sent magazines, books, reports, articles, and news releases from which this material is gleaned. A special thanks to Reuben and Jenny Schweiger who served as my "sounding boards" during the development of the manuscript and to my secretary Sydney Boggs who typed the manuscript. A deep appreciation and love go to members of my family who have continually supported my work in the ministry and my sojourns to Africa.

—Jane Heaton
June 1, 1982

African church.

"In no other continent during the last 50 years has Christianity shown so much growth and diversity."

A Century Of Growth

by Adrian Hastings

The Christian churches are today thriving in Africa as almost nowhere else. The era of "mission"—in which Christianity in Africa was seen as a plant which had hardly taken root, which needed constant care from outside, which it was a duty to instruct but to which one would certainly not expect to listen—that era is over!

Today there are at least 90 million (statistics vary) Christians on the continent of Africa and the number is steadily growing. The Copts in Egypt and the Orthodox Church in Ethiopia continue as they have done for over 1500 years. The Roman Catholic Church has more than 300 dioceses across the length and breadth of Africa. Anglicans, Lutherans, Methodists, Presbyterians, Baptists, Pentecostals, all have strong churches in one or another part of the continent. Then there are the new denominations—Kimbanguists and Aladura, Eden Revival and Maria Legio, Zionists and Ethiopians, Prophetic churches, praying churches, healing churches. They have all been founded by Africans during the last 100 years and now have millions of adherents of their own.

What riches and complexity are to be found here:

—the life and death of the Zairean prophet Simon Kimbangu;

—the lonely witness of Lambarene hospital in Gabon of that ascetic but obstinate theologian, musician and doctor, Albert Schweitzer;

—the communist-capitalist success story of the 'Happy City,' the Holy Apostles Community at Aiyetoro in a Nigerian coastal lagoon;

—the World Council grants to African Liberation Movements and the emergence of black theology;

—philosopher leaders such as Leopold Senghor and Julius Nyerere;

—the heroically consistent and restrained witness against

1

apartheid of the Dutch Reformed Predikant Beyers Naude.

The modern African church has had its prophets and visionaries, its kings and its priests, its strategists, its martyrs, its vociferous spokespersons, its innumerable humble worshipers.

It is safe to say that in no other continent during the last 50 years has Christianity shown so much growth and diversity, such a cheerful but perplexing flood of people confidently doing their own thing, often in seemingly strange and contradictory ways. And yet, just 100 years ago, African Christianity only barely existed. In 1875, it is true, the state church of Ethiopia and the Coptic Church of Egypt were already as old and venerable as any church throughout the world, but they were in no way in contact with the rest of the continent. Elsewhere there were a few Christian communities scattered along the coasts of Africa, particularly in the south and west, but most inland parts had never known the gospel preached in any form.

The Spread of Christianity

On the West Coast from Senegal to the Niger River a network of sturdy little churches, Anglican, Methodist, Presbyterian and Catholic, now existed. There were the fruit of black Christians returning from the Americas, and of the brief efforts of white missionaries from Europe destined in nearly every case for an early grave. The people who really carried the Christian faith along the West Coast in the mid-19th century were nearly all Africans, many of them men and women rescued from slave ships on the Atlantic and landed by the British navy at Freetown. For example, Lott Carey, a former slave from Virginia, helped establish Baptist work in Liberia and ended up helping to establish the nation of Liberia. Carey was important in the emergence of Liberia as an independent black nation which has never been colonized.

One of the most remarkable of the pioneer missionaries was never a slave, though his father had been. Thomas Birch Freeman had a Negro father and an English mother. Born in England, his 50 years of service on the Gold Coast—began at time when most of his fellow missionaries lived only a year or so. Freeman did much to establish Methodism as the most deeply rooted church of southern Ghana.

The best known Christian pioneer of that age was undoubtedly Samuel Ajayi Crowther. A Yoruba, he was rescued as a boy at 15 from a slave ship in 1822, was educated by Anglican missionaries in Freetown and then himself became a teacher at their college of Fourah bay before returning to his own country of Nigeria as a missionary. In 1864 he was consecrated as a bishop in Cantebury Cathedral—the first African bishop of the Anglican communion. His diocese was vast, the whole of West Africa outside the small existing British colonies being initially entrusted to him, though in fact he concentrated on the lower Niger. But as the white missionaries were not willing to serve under him they continued to be responsible to the English Bishop of Sierre Leone. Eleven years later, in May 1875, one elderly missionary, David Hinderer, wrote: "Has not the time come when the native bishop's jurisdiction should be further extended than the Niger, especially to his own native soil?"

However, the tide was to flow the other way. Despite Crowther's patient and conscientious work across the years, white missionaries both on the spot and in England increasingly distrusted him, believing that his appointment had been essentially a mistake. The reins of power should be kept firmly in efficient white hands for an indefinite period. At the time most missionaries tended to despise both African culture and African capacity. They believed that the Christian religion must go with a western culture and western leadership. Already African Christians were becoming conscious of this contempt, resented it and frequently saw the future of African Christianity in a very different way.

By 1875 there was an African Christian society along the West Coast, from the Catholic Church in Senegal at one end to Bishop Crowther's diocese on the lower Niger at the other. In southern Africa too, besides the white settler churches—Dutch Reformed, Anglican, Methodist—in the western Cape, Grahamstown and on the high grazing areas, missionaries had been active for many years among some Africans not only on the coast but far inland.

Robert Moffat, of the London Missionary Society and David Livingstone's father-in-law, was the great pioneer north of the Orange River. From his headquarters at Kuruman he traveled widely over what is now Botswana and Zimbabwe. French Evangelicals and Roman Catholics vied with one another among the Basuto people in their mountains while nearer the coast churches were multiplying particularly among the Xhosa people. By 1875 the great Khama, baptized 12 years before, was chief of the Bamangwato. The pride of the London Missionary Society, he was to establish the dominance of Congregationalism and abstinence from alcohol among his people in what is now Botswana.

Four years before, in September 1871, Tiyo Soga, the Presbyterian, first minister of the Xhosa people, had died from fever contracted during his pastoral journeying. Educated for some years in Scotland, he had become a superb writer of hymns, the translater of *Pilgrim's Progress* as well as parts of the Bible, and a singularly ecumenical figure. He was known as an untiring preacher and pastor, a lover of all persons whatever their denomination, a renowned master of language and the pride of his people. As witness to African Christianity a century ago he stands for the south as Crowther stands for the west.

Further north there was almost nothing. The old Portuguese missions on both the west coast and the east had almost disappeared by this time, leaving behind a few buildings, many of them more or less in ruins, and a pitiful handful of clergy to minister to the small white or half-white colonial population. Livingstone died in 1873 in the northern part of what is now Zambia and next to nothing has been done to spread the gospel to the heart of Africa beyond a few coastal mission stations— the Anglicans at Mombasa, the Holy Ghost Fathers at Bagamoyo.

The expedition of the Universities Mission to Central Africa led by Bishop Mackenzie to the Lower Shire in the early 1860s had been forced quickly to withdraw after Mackenzie's death. Yet 1875 was to be the most significant date for the start of a new penetration. It was the year in which a Scottish Presbyterian party set out to establish the mission of Livingstonia on the shores of Lake Malawi. It included Robert Laws who was to be the presiding genius of Livingstonia, perhaps the most decisively influential institution in the whole of that part of Africa, and he would still be at work there in the 1930s.

In 1875 the Universities Mission to Central Africa decided that the time was ripe for a new venture to the interior and struck inland from Zanzibar to Magila in the hill country of northern Tanzania. Two years later the first Anglican missionaries reached the court of King Mutesa of Buganda to be followed within a few months by the White Fathers of Cardinal Lavigerie.

Fifty years later—1925

That is how Christianity stood in Africa over one hundred years ago: resolute beginnings but little more. If we now turn

4

over 50 years and look at the scene again in 1925, what do we find? In the meantime the European powers—Great Britain, France, Belgium, Portugal and, until the first world war, Germany—divided almost the entire continent between them. In 1875 Africa was a continent of hundreds of independent kingdoms, tribes, small republics, coastal colonies—an intricate political chaos.

By 1925 the heavy hand colonialism has sorted out all that, establishing at the same time a network of railways and roads which made the task of the missionary much less difficult. And the churches had spread almost as much as the empires. There were now some 7,000 Roman Catholic and 5,500 Protestant missionaries in Africa south of the Sahara, while the number of Christians was some five million as against perhaps half a million 50 years before. If the whole population was something in the order of 150 million in 1925, then about 3 percent was now Christian, and the number was growing fast. There were large areas, particularly those regarded as Muslim such as northern Nigeria where missionaries were hardly permitted to enter, but the accessible field before them was now vast indeed.

By 1975 African Christianity was looking very different from how it had looked in 1925. First of all, the political situation had again changed radically. The colonial system so very settled in 1925 had by 1975 faded away almost everywhere. The young men and women of Nigeria or Zaire can hardly remember a time when their country was not independent. The five million Christians of 1925 were now some 90 million. The number of churches, dioceses, missions, even foreign missionaries, had all vastly grown. Even if the missionary force had somewhat decreased since 1965, it was still more than three times as numerous as it was in 1925—40,000 in place of 12,000.

In the 1920s there was everywhere something of a surface calm, though the emergence of so many prophetic figures at that time and the great welcome they received suggest that, in the souls of many, things were far from tranquil. There was already a deep conflict between two patterns of life, old and new, within which ordinary Africans found themselves torn apart. Fifty years later all the tension had come to the surface. Political independence proved the arena for the reassertion both of new and old. The formal eradication of colonialism had been in truth the takeover of the European system basically unchanged by an African elite trained in a European way to run European conceived government, economy and educational systems. In a sense the recipe of post-independence Africa has been no more complex than "the same but more of it." On the other side the slogans of independence have proved the stimulus for a collective reexamination of the presuppositions of society and its sense of direction. This critique is not one that can be carried on in tranquility. The pressures of the population explosion, poverty, rapid urbanization, the breakdown of that very machinery of government which the new elite inherited from the colonial powers, all this has created such a crisis of society that even a hardened well-wisher can ask despairingly—"Can Africa survive?"

The churches are caught up in every side of the tension. They may as well be rejected by the Marxist innovator as by the traditionalist insisting upon African "authenticity." They may be identified with the privileged rich elite, with patterns of neo-colonialism, but also with the underprivileged masses struggling for freedom, regional autonomy or simply protesting against the corruption of their masters. Nearly all of them are, far more clearly than in earlier decades, African churches. Almost all the leaders of the mission-connected churches are now African, the remaining missionaries playing in most places an increasingly subsidiary role. From this point of view the gap between "mission" churches and "independent" churches has diminished. But this does not mean that mission-linked churches can now always brush off the charge of being an alien element without difficulty. Much about them remains undoubtedly alien, even unnecessarily alien. Yet so is very much else in modern Africa, and inevitably. The character of the churches and their leadership often harmonize only too well with the character of contemporary society and the leadership in other areas of life.

Christian Leaders

The political, intellectual and business leaders of today's Africa have come largely from the same stable. They too are mostly Christians, except in the predominantly Muslim areas; they went through the church schools and are often closely linked by blood or friendship with the ecclesiastical leaders. Leopold Senghor, the first president of Senegal, studied in a seminary. Zambia president Kaunda's father was a Presbyterian minister. The brother-in-law of the first president of the Republic of Kenya, Kenyatta, is a priest. Nyerere, Tanzania's first president, likes nothing more than to sit down and argue things out with a bench of bishops. The church's fate and public image depend as much upon these men as upon the purely ecclesiastical leadership.

The Church's Involvement in Political Conflicts

The churches could not possibly remain uninvolved in the political conflicts which have swept across Africa—their members are fully caught up in them and generally on more than one side. Christians were profoundly committed to one of the two parties in the Nigerian civil war. They provided the greater part of the Southern Leadership in the Sudanese civil war. They were predominant among both Batutsi and Bahutu in the bitter tribal conflicts of Burundi and Rwanda. They have taken every point of view in regard to the racial conflicts of the south. Cardinal Malula had to go into temporary exile after challenging President Mobutu at the start of the "authenticity" campaign in Zaire, while in many other countries, bishops, priests and numerous members of the congregations have been imprisoned, exiled and killed.

Three Christians murdered in 1972 may stand for the many who have suffered in the conflicts of this period. Father Michel Kayoya, a Hutu, was a brilliant young priest in Burundi. He was the author of two very beautiful books, *My Father's Footprints* and *Between Two Worlds,* in which he discussed the relations between African tradition, humanism, Marxism and Christianity, and criticized the craving for money, social parasitism and legal insecurity of modern Burundi. In the wake of the Hutu rebellion he was arrested and shot without trial on May 17 at a bridge over the Rububu River. He was buried in a common grave with some 7,000 other victims.

In September 1972 the Chief Justice of Uganda, Benedicto Kiwanuka, was suddenly seized and never seen in public again. Benedicto was a devout Catholic and a good family man, a lawyer of integrity and the country's first prime minister. He had been in prison for years under Amin's predecessor Obote, was released by Amin, and made chief justice. But he had then courageously used his position to temper his country's increasingly illegal and bloodthirsty tyranny. He paid the price of a terrible death, being dismembered alive in the military prison of

Makindye. He was only one, if the most distinguished, among thousands of victims.

In June 1972 a large number of Protestant church leaders in Mozambique were suddenly arrested by the dreaded Portuguese political police and imprisoned in the concentration camp of Machava. Among them was Zedequias Manganhela, president of the Presbyterian synodal council, an elderly pastor, a family man in his sixties. In the subsequent months he and his fellows were ruthlessly interrogated day after day in an attempt to establish links between the protestant churches and the Mozambique Liberation Front (Frelimo). Then one morning, December 11, Manganhela was found hanged in his prison cell, again one victim among very many of the racial tyranny and police brutality of southern Africa.

Kiwanuka the lawyer and politician, Kayoya the brilliant young priest-author, Manganhela the quiet humorous old pastor—these can stand for many persons who are victims of black oppression as well as white, tribal and racial conflicts, man's inhumanity to man. Nevertheless the dominant impression of these years is not one of persecution and martyrdom. It is rather one of growth, success and increasing self-confidence.

The Stability of the African Church

In 1950, some people were asking themselves what would happen to the churches in Africa once European rule was brought to an end. Clearly the churches came to most parts of the continent within the wide context of colonial expansion. The two movements were often closely linked. There was no alternative. But if that was so, might not the two end together as well? Or, at least, would not the churches greatly decline once African political independence was achieved? It can now be seen that such questions derived from a deep misunderstanding of the depth to which Africans both in the "mission" and in the "independent" churches had made Christianity their own. In fact, all in all, the post-independence years have been ones of almost spectacular ecclesiastical advance.

The problem of the Christian churches in Africa today are many and deep, but they are seldom problems of decline. They arise instead from the sheer rapidity of growth, from an almost discordant vitality. They arise from the need, and often to the determination, to reshape the pattern of church life and thought learned directly or indirectly from western missionaries to be in accord with the complex religious and secular needs of African society, while remaining faithful to the essentials of Christian tradition. While many of the problems are ones which in some way or another affect other parts of the world church, their specifically African character remains very strong and it is as such that we want to understand them.

Reprinted with permission from *African Christianity,* by Adrian Hastings (Geoffrey Chapman: Lomdon and Dublin, 1976) pp. 1-5, 13-16. Edited for this publication.

Carvings from thorn bush, a traditional form of art.

"There are an estimated 100 million Black Christians in Africa today. Predictions are there will be at least 50 million more by the year 2000."

Africa's Christian Revolution

Almost from the beginning of time, it seems, Africa has been caught in the painful grip of revolution. About 31 years ago Africa was still almost totally "owned" by colonial powers. Britain, then still an empire, had fourteen colonies and protectorates. French Africa covered almost a third of the continent. Portugal, Belgium and Italy had the rest. Only five nations, Liberia, Libya, Egypt, Ethiopia and South Africa, were considered free.

Most of Africa is free today—a freedom bought by numerous revolutions and much bloodshed and sorrow. A person relatively aware of events in Africa could ask, with some justification: Aside from the conflicts in Namibia (South West Africa) and South Africa and the continent's struggle against a world economic system which favors wealthy nations—aside from all this what else is there in Africa to talk about?

Well, although this is not absolutely new information, another revolution is going on in Africa, especially in black Africa south of the Sahara. It is not being fought with guns and lethal weapons this time. No one is dying. It's a revolution, nevertheless, one for and not against people. A revolution characterized by the positive force of love.

The Growth of Christianity

This "other" revolution is the phenomenal rate of growth of Christianity in Africa.

No one can say with certainty how many Black Christians there were in Africa 150 years ago. Surely, say mission historians, both Roman Catholic and Protestant missionaries had arrived on the continent before 1833. But, not many Africans had come to know the Lord Jesus Christ as the divine and only Savior or had become his disciples.

Now the growth of Christianity in Africa is unparalleled anywhere in the world. An estimated 100 million black Christians

Some Thoughts About African Theology

Describing a theology which is still taking shape is difficult. Instead of giving a completed picture of African theology this article consists of information from various books and articles by African theologians. It explores some of the problems involved in the development of an African theology and some of the developing concepts as an African theology continues to take shape.

Why A Special African Theology?

First of all, no theological thought is completely final or perfect. Of course, the true insights of theological thought must have universal relevance, but it becomes distorted if it sets out to speak universally. And unity arises because ultimately all are reflecting on the one divine activity which aims to set individuals free from all that enslaves them. There must be a plurality of theologies because not everyone apprehends the transcendent in exactly the same way no is that experience expressed in the same way.

The second factor—or problem—facing African theologians is stated by S. Nomenyo in his article on "Theology in the Life of the Churches."

"What we understand by African theology is something that we ourselves must define clearly, unaffected by outside desires and wishes, but under the guidance of the Holy Spirit. Are we to remain slaves to patterns and models set up in the West for theology and the theologian, or shall we be set free to create our own patterns and models?

"Today in Africa there is an intense need for an intervention of the Lord:

—to free the Christians of our continent of undue attachment to this or that "confession of faith" or denomination, in order to make them one Church of the living Christ who is present and active in their societies, so that they may be truly and fully human beings and have life in abundance.

—to make of them communities of men and women, young and adult, of all ethnic groups and social strata, who will live face-to-face with God in Jesus Christ, feeling that God has taken charge of them absolutely, for their past, present and future life, and living no longer for themselves but for him who died and rose for them.

—who will make of us his people, where all of us are taught by him, advancing together in mutual respect, support and enrichment, committed together to one mission in common with Christ.

"We await a Church for our continent where all the members will have ingrained in them the vital and unshaken certainty that he who was misunderstood, despised, hated, rejected and crucified is indeed he whom God sent in to the world to free people from all their fears, from all their enemies and from all that makes for oppression, servitude and alienation, so that they may live in his presence, in freedom, love, truth and justice, all the days of their lives.

"Our theological work should serve as an instrument for this intervention of the Lord of the Church. It will then be at the service of a Christian life with its source in Christ and expressing itself and flourishing in the African way of life."

Emphasis on Life as the Supreme Good

To the African mind, life is the supreme good. Life is sacred. All beings which inhabit the world—plant, animal, human and spiritual—receive life from God and bear within them the principle of life. Life is like a vital current originating in the supreme being and spreading to all creation. To live, in the case of women and men, means to participate in this current as a whole, with the task of lifting it to its source. It means participation, first on the level of the plant world, then the animal, then the spiritual, and finally on the level of the Supreme Being. This makes relationship important: relations between peoples and nature, between individuals persons and all people, between peoples and the spirits. Everything that promotes this participation is good. Evil, on the other hand, is all that runs counter to life, all that destroys relationships, all that separates, divides and estranges. To communicate life—to transmit it, to protect it, to defend it—is good. To destroy it is evil.

In the light of this the African theologian must weigh and understand African life.

The African theologian is confronted with the challenges posed by the traditional customs of African society. How can the Christian community contribute by its presence, its testimony and its style of social life to the functioning of the forces which make for unity, solidarity, sharing and support? For protection against evil and disintegration? For dissuasion in the face of actions which destroy values and human relationship? For encouragement to do good?

How can the Christian community help to discern behind these forces God's will for humans? How can it work for their development, their improvement and their transformation? To be "the salt of the earth," to be "a Church for others" and, especially, to be "the light of the world"—what does all this imply for the Christian community of Africa?

From *African Challenge.*

The Contribution of Traditional Religion

"The God described in the Bible is none other than the God who is already known in the framework of traditional African religiosity. The missionaries who introduced the gospel to Africa in the past 200 years did not bring God to that continent. Instead God brought them. They proclaimed the name of Jesus Christ. But they used the names of the God who was and is already known by African peoples—such as Mungu, Mulungu, Katonda, Ngai, Olodumare, Asis, Ruwa, Ruhanga, Jok, Modimo, Unkulunkulu and thousands more. These were not empty names. They were names of the one and the same God, the creator of the world, the Father of our Lord Jesus Christ.

"No doubt much research and reflection remain to be done in order to work out a consistent theological understanding of the issues here. The truth seems to be that God's revelation is not confined to the biblical record. One important task, then, is to see the nature, the method and the implications of God's revelation among African peoples, in the light of the biblical record of the same revelation.

"The rapid spreading of the Christian faith where people

have been predominantly followers of African religion pro-vokes interesting questions. That which had been seen as the enemy of the gospel turns out to be indeed a welcoming friend. African religion has equipped people to listen to the gospel, to discover meaningful passages in the Bible, and to avoid unhealthy religious conflict.

"Theological development in Africa must inevitably grow within this religious setting.

"For this reason, some African theologians take African religiosity to be one of the sources of theological reflection. A conference of mainly African theologians, held in Ghana in December 1977, said in its final communique:

"The God of history speaks to all peoples in particular ways. In Africa the traditional religions are a major source for the study of the African experience of God. The beliefs and practices of the traditional religions in Africa can enrich Christian theology and spirituality.

"The church is composed largely of people who come out of the African religious background. Their culture, history, world views and spiritual aspirations cannot be taken away from them. These impinge upon their daily life and experience of the Christian faith. So the church which exists on the African scene bears the marks of its people's backgrounds. No viable theology can grow in Africa without addressing itself to the inter-religious phenomenon at work there."

—John Mbiti, from an article in *The Christian Century*.

Central Place of the Bible

African Christianity has the Bible at its forefront, and the Bible is shaping much of its development both explicitly and implicitly. Oral theology, which is largely a prerequisite to written theology, is also strongly grounded in the scriptures. As long as African theology keeps close to the scriptures, it will remain relevant to the life of the churches of Africa and it will have lasting links with the theology of the church universal.

Edward Fashole-Luke is right in reminding us that "the Bible is the basic primary source for the development of African Christian theologies." Nothing can substitute for the Bible. However much African cultural-religious background may be close to the biblical word Africans need to guard against reference like "the hitherto unwritten African Old Testament" or sentiments that see a final revelation of God in the African religious heritage.

African theologians must give even more attention to the Bible than is sometimes the case. As long as the Bible is kept close to minds and hearts, African theology will be viable, relevant, and of lasting service to the church and glory to the Lord to whom be honor, dominion and power until ages of ages.

From article by John Mbiti in the *International Bulletin of Missionary Research.*

African Concern for Wholeness

The African theological contribution is not in any way restricted to the insights of the non-Christian religious tradition of Africa. As already stated, theology must be contemporary and must derive from modern cultural life. Nevertheless, ancient religious ideas are highly resilient in the modern situations.

An area in which Africa can probably make a contribution is in the realm of the so-called secular theology. Secularism is often wrongly assumed to be the final phase in movement towards a more developed technology. But it has nothing inherently to do with modern living or with the scientific discoveries of this age. The most common experience of Africa has been religious, but religion that is fully integrated with every aspect of individual and social life. This integration was so far-reaching that some scholars have concluded that African traditional religion was weakened by being world-centered and pragmatic. This view probably reflects a western dichotomy between sacred and profane, spirit and matter, supernatural and natural. African theologians might help the world rediscover the relativity of such terms as "sacred" and "profane" and encourage the typically African vision of "wholeness" or integration.

—Aylward Shorter, British Missionary

17

The Value of Life

Another theme is that of fecundity. Africans place great value on physical generation, on life, and the sharing of life. Fundamentally this is because of their humanity and their esteem for interpersonal relationships. In the western world "the good life" has been equated with mechanical ingenuity, with labor-saving devices, with the easier and cheaper manufacture of household goods and luxuries. Such an equation is ultimately dehumanizing.

True progress does not exalt mechanical ingenuity over personal values. If technology is in itself good as a means of sharing in the creativity of God, then personal values must be preserved in a technologically developed world. Africa has not yet felt the full impact of western technology. Perhaps Africa will never be as heavily industrialized and urbanized as other parts of the world. On the other hand, even in the rural areas, Africa is feeling the effects of a profound social revolution. Perhaps Africans may be no more successful than westerners in preventing a technological society from becoming impersonal and enslaving. On the other hand, African theologians might assist in a process of reevaluation.

—Aylward Shorter, British Missionary

NEW ASSOCIATION FOR AFRICAN THEOLOGY CREATED

The promotion of African theology, a better cooperation between theologians of different countries, languages and cultures in Africa as well as a better circulation of specialized publications and a real theological dialogue will be some of the aims of the new Ecumenical Association of African Theologians (EAAT). The organization officially came into being at the first general assembly, Sept. 24-28, 1980, in Yaounde, Cameroun, where a constitution was approved and an executive committee elected.

The creation of EAAT grew from an initiative taken by African theologians of various denominations during the Second Congress of the Ecumenical Association of Third World Theologians in Accra, Ghana, in 1977.

The EAAT will support theological seminaries and consultations and publicize theological studies made in various African countries in its African Theological Bulletin.

What Do You Need To Be A Chief?

THE GREAT CHIEF of a tribal kingdom had only one son. Because he had only one son, it was very important that he train him well. Someday this boy would take his place. If he trained him poorly and the boy was not a good chief, his people would not remember him kindly. If the boy ruled well, the people would have happy memories of his father.

So all the years while the boy was growing up, his father tried to prepare him for his future. Finally the day came for the chief to test his son, as was the custom.

He took his bag of magic medicines, a hoe and his son, and went on a journey into the forest. The father and the boy walked down the trail together until they reached the thick dark center of the jungle. There they came to a clearing. In the center of the clearing the father took the hoe and dug a large circle in the ground. He put the boy in the center of it. Then he said, "My child, no matter what happens, you must not leave this circle until I come for you again. Do you understand?"

"Yes, I understand," answered the boy. The father left the clearing and hid in the forest nearby to watch.

The boy sat down on the ground to wait. He felt terribly alone and afraid. He wondered what had happened to his father. Soon he heard a rustling sound in the underbrush. He strained his ears to hear where it was coming from. Then he saw something coming toward him. It was a big black snake!

The boy jumped up, ready to run. Then he remembered the words of his father: "My child, you must not leave this circle until I come for you again." He could not disobey his father; so he sat down again.

The snake came closer and closer until it reached the edge of the circle. It fastened its beady eyes on the boy, shifting its head slowly from side to side as if it were going to strike him. Then something seemed to change its mind, and it slowly turned and went away.

The boy sat in the quietness for what seemed like a long time. Then he was terrified by the roar of a lion. It roared again so fiercely that it shook the tree branches. Chills of fear raced down the boy's backbone. What would he do if the lion found him? Should he run away?

Then the boy saw the lion's flaming eyes peer at him from under the bushes. Suddenly the lion gave a great leap toward him, and landed on the very edge of the circle. He prowled around its edge growling. The boy turned and turned with the lion, keeping his eyes on it all the time. Finally the lion gave a great roar of anger, turned, and went back into the forest.

The sun was getting low in the sky; the jungle was becoming dark. Still the father had not come back. The boy was lonesome, hungry and terribly afraid. Had his father forgotten him? Maybe he would never return.

Then the boy smelled something strange. He heard dry branches crackling. He turned to look, and sure enough, he saw the flames of a forest fire. The flames came closer and closer. They jumped high into the treetops and heaved great billows of black smoke into the sky. Should he run? No, he would stay even if he burned up.

The flames came closer and closer until the fire was so hot he could hardly breathe. But when the flames reached the edge of the circle, they began to die down, until finally they went out, leaving the ground all around him black and smoking.

Then from the edge of the jungle came his father. How happy the boy was to see him! The father gathered the boy into his arms and said, "Son, you are a very brave and obedient boy. I sent the snake and the lion and the fire. I wanted to try you. You have proven yourself. You will become a worthy chief when I die. Let us return to the village."

The young boy was now sure that if he kept obeying and trusting his father, everything would come out all right.

From *African Fables* (Scottdale, Pa.: Herald Press, 1978), p. 79.)

BANTU WISDOM

Carve with your friend, alone you cut yourself.

Consultation On Church Music

After years of discussion on the indigenization of African music and worship, the All Africa Conference of Churches (AACC) under the leadership of the Rev. Richard Rakotondraibe of the Department of Faith and Identity of the Church took action. Five regional consultations were held during 1980-82 across the African continent—southern Africa, East Africa, Northeast Africa, English-speaking West Africa and all French-speaking Africa and Madagascar. Following the regional consultations, a Pan-African consultation was held in Lome, Togo, April 11-17, 1981, to pull together the recommendations of the regional consultations.

The objectives of the consultations were stated as follows:

—To engage in deep reflection on every aspect of African religious music and the factors which have influenced it.

—To discuss means whereby African churches can be sensitized to its importance and potential.

—To promote an exchange of experiences in different countries and churches, which would enrich the research on African religious music, sharing the successes as well as the failures.

—To work towards the eventual publication of an international hymnal which would include a large percentage of hymns written by Africans, with an African style and that innate feeling expressed in a particular harmony, movement and rhythm.

African Church Music

by Donald Bobb

For three years, my wife and I attended church services in Lome, Togo, and other cities in West Africa. We grew accustomed to the ever-changing style of the worship. An increasing number of choirs were formed in each congregation, dispersed throughout the sanctuary, and sang at designated moments during the worship. Often choir members would use gestures to give more meaning to their singing. The women and girls might dramatize in pantomime scenes such as the joy of Mary at the Annunciation, the perplexity of the women at the Empty Tomb or themes such as the Christian sorrowing, sympathizing or rejoicing.

At times some choir members would quietly start moving into the aisles, gently swaying to the rhythm of the music. Offering plates would remain on the altar, while the participants at worship filed up to the front to place their offerings in the plates. Tam-tams (drums) would give additional impetus to the music sung by choir and congregation, thrilling the worshipers of Togo much as the great pipe organ thrills worshipers of Europe and North America.

An outstanding renewal in African worship is taking place today. Guitars, cymbals, triangles, tam-tams and homemade, ingenious percussion instruments such as pieces of metal or bottles have replaced the pump organ and piano. But this renewal is far from being complete. Western music and forms still prevail. While African authenticity and faithfulness to traditional roots is the predominant force in African society today, there is hesitancy on the part of church leadership to move too far away from the "imported roots" of western Christianity for fear of deteriorating into the traditional faith and practices, considered "paganistic" and still strongly present in African life.

Theologians have begun to extract from African traditional religion those elements which help implant the Christian gospel in African culture. This movement towards Africanization prevails in the church—whether it pertains to theology, church discipline, church polity, relationships between church and society, relationships within the church community, or worship and music.

For decades, the African church has been called to worship by the church bell, sung "imported" hymns to the accompaniment of piano or organ, and tried to sit motionless on the long, often backless, benches. Christians had been taught by the early missionaries that the harp and drums were vehicles of paganism and that bodily movements could lead to diabolical manifestations. With the years of independence has come change that is authentically African beginning to assert itself. It is time for the old melodies, the highly intricate rhythms and the accompanying movements of the body and feet to become as natural an expression of Christian worship as they were for traditional ceremonial and religious celebrations.

During a recent consultation on church music, lectures were given on the identity of traditional music, as it related to life in society; movements in the worship service; musical instruments and their place in worship; and the choir and its music as a means of communication. Workshops were organized along more practical lines:

—transcription of melodies and rhythms into sol-fa notations or musical notes;

—the harmonious use of hymns, instruments and movement;

—listening to hymns from different countries in view of preparing the all African hymnal;

—and an attempt at an adaptation of the liturgy into a more African idiom.

Bible studies revealed the solid biblical foundation for a variety of instrumental worship expressions (Psalm 150), for the use of dance (2 Samuel 6) and the validity of authentic cultural traditions. (Acts 17:26-7; Rom. 12:1) The African's interpretation of music in the universe differs from that of the westerner, who places more emphasis on tonal development and quality than on the rhythm and movement so dominant in African music.

According to Seth Kwadzo of Lome, Togo, "traditional music is based above all . . . .on a system of oral transmission. . . .from generation to generation, a tradition which must serve as link between the past and the present." He talks of the relationship between music and rhythm: "Rhythm is a natural element. . . .the foundation, the essential element whose importance is as great as that of sound." Rhythm then leads to a further development, because when "movement" is added to "rhythm" the result is "dance."

Rev. Richard Rakotondraibe had divided the development of African church music into four periods, which also serve as a typology of hymns:

1) the period of importation, when both word and melody were imported from Europe and America;

2) the period of adaptation, when the music was imported from the West, but the words were composed by Africans;

3) the period of imitation, when both words and music were composed by Africans, but the music was an imitation of a western melody; and

4) the period of authentic creativity, when both the words and music are composed by Africans, according to values and standards authentically African.

Within African life, music fulfills several functions. It stimulates work. It serves as a means of distraction. It prepares the people for hunting and for war. It occupies a central position in ceremonial occasions of important life events.

Music is used for work at home, in the fields, in the forests, on the rivers and on lakes or oceans. Music helps people to forget the monotony of their labors and the difficulty of their tasks. It helps to coordinate their efforts with their companions in order to bring about the best results. Music increases production, diminishes fatigue, and offers distraction for those who sing as well as for those who listen.

Traditional music plays an important role in social life. Especially in those places where ancestral customs are still maintained—in traditional religious ceremonies pertaining to marriage, birth and death, in agricultural labor, in political meetings and receptions. It may be vocal or instrumental, sung by a single person or a choral group. Horns, flutes, harps and other locally made instruments give tone to the best of the tam-tam.

The times have changed. Science and technology have eliminated some arduous tasks. Bicycles, buses and trains do not encourage poetic or musical inspiration. Modern systems of irrigation have suppressed songs chanted during the carrying of water. Tractors have replaced the cultivator, the hand cultivation and the music accompanying that effort. Transistor radios have invaded the most inaccessible regions displacing the local singers and entertainment groups. Urban residents go more and more to the movies or watch television rather than attend concerts or plays. Rural residents imitate musicians heard on the radio rather than sing in the ancestral manner. Music creativity seems to be slowing down and the artistic level of popular music is lowering.

All of the great achievements of the African musical heritage are gradually disappearing because of the invasion of western culture. Two cultures have come into confrontation—foreign instruments, imported singing style, choral harmony, different scale of tones—creating a hybrid music. As Kwadzo says, "Every people finds real joy in making its music. . . .Our duty is to discover how to preserve our traditional music and our instruments."

African church music has approached the hybrid mixture from the "imported" direction and now is struggling to be at least "hybrid" if not totally indigenous. Popular melodies in the West were absorbed into the western church and given religious words. Slowly the same socio-religious phenomenon is occurring in Africa. It is being encouraged and stimulated in ways that will not produce shock waves of accusations for fears of "paganism" entering the church, but in ways that will arouse the sensual awareness of worshipers. They will feel the rhythm and find expression in the movement of clapping hands, swaying body and quiet tapping feet.

In order to achieve this preservation of the great African musical tradition and promote a modern evolution of its nature and forms, many recommendations have been proposed. Church musicians are urged to study carefully the works of African musicologists to see what is happening to music in Africa. In turn, church musicians and theologians/pastors can determine more aptly the trends and directions they feel Christian music can take. The goal is for it to portray African "feeling" and at the same time proclaim and embody the gospel message.

Every congregation should have a choir, whose members are trained and prepared for their ministry through music. They need to understand what they are singing and that they live out and preach the gospel through their music. The members should remain African in style and dress and in the use of movement and instruments, without rejecting or forgetting the universality of the church. Programs and concerts should be organized for neighborhoods and villages. In addition choirs can sing at ceremonial occasions—to bring comfort to a bereaved family during mourning ceremonies or to bring joy to a young couple during wedding celebrations.

A renewal in liturgy is encouraged, which would include quiet meditation, use of instruments, cooperation between composers of "inspired religious songs" and theologians or pastors, use of movement during worship, clerical and choral robes with an African motif, the most accommodating position for private and congregational prayer, and a deeper study of the sacraments, their meaning and their efficacy.

A hymn book for all churches in Africa is being prepared, which will include some of the more favored western hymns and some African hymns widely representative of the continent as a whole. The hymns would be printed in English, French and the African language in which the hymn was written.

Furthermore it has been proposed that an All African Association of Religious Music be created under the auspices of the All Africa Conference of Churches. National and regional music associations should be created and the AACC should offer its moral support in the development of these local associations in the various churches and countries. The church leadership is quite frequently stubborn in its opposition to the introduction of African music and expression into the worship service. Hence, the support of the AACC is essential in such cases.

The musicians present at recent consultations all agreed that it is urgent to recover the esteem for African religious music before it is too late. Cultural egotism must be avoided. At the same time, objective and positive values of the African musical heritage must be preserved. As Kwadzo told his African audience:

"Wherever they are singing traditional music, take your place and listen; you will discover, not only joy but also many other mysterious things."

The beginning of baldness is the thinning above the temples.

"The Christian message is always the same, but every new convert teaches us more of its meaning."

A Perspective In Missions To Africa In The '80s

by Ajayi E. Nicol

It is becoming increasingly evident that most of those who today engage in missions to the so-called Third World, especially Africa, have lost the intent and vision of missionary enterprise as was commissioned by our Lord. For people like David Livingstone and others like him, it was a matter of life and death—"there was no other name under heaven whereby humanity could be saved, save that of Jesus" whose instruction to Christians is "ye shall be my witnesses."

Because of my various jobs with the church in Africa, I have lived and traveled in many parts of the African continent for at least a minimum of a week and during those periods I had close contact with church leaders. Therefore with some humility I could say that I have experienced some of the missionary activities currently going on in the continent.

It seems to have become a symbol of prestige to have a mission station somewhere in Africa as is evident by the denominational rivalries that the continent has been witnessing. This mission activity seems to be carried out as an act of self-engrandizement rather than of service and witness in the name of Christ.

It is worth noting that Africa in the past experienced Apostolic Christianity in Egypt and Ethiopia and produced such church leaders as Tertullian, Augustine and Cyprian, whose influence on western Christian theology could not be forgotten. Our Lord, in fact, found refuge in Egypt for years.

In modern times one could safely say that the rest of the continent has had over a century of Christian experience through the missionary activities of the 1800s. Ironically all the history books on the continent begin with the coming of the colonial powers and/or missionaries as though no one existed before then.

The major input of the missionary enterprise together with

Christianity included health, education and western cultural values. All of which we have been grateful for in Africa. But today we are beginning to realize that some of these values are rather repressive. In order to enforce western cultural values the missionaries had adopted the policy of the "clean slate," through which everything that was African was condemned as being "pagan." What is pagan about a piece of skin placed over wood—a drum? As a matter of fact, at no time has the African been pagan in the true sense of the word. Africans had always worshiped the Supreme Divine through intermediaries because in our culture one does not take one's petitions directly to the Chief save through an intermediary. And since the Supreme Divine was conceived as the great Spirit, none could reach that Spirit but lesser spirits—the departed ancestors and those found in extraordinary trees, rivers and rocks. This was done in ignorance for sure, but that was not to say that these media were worshiped in themselves. The missionaries who did not understand this, without making any effort to learn what was going on, condemned it outright as idolatry, thus branding the Africans as pagans.

As mentioned above we did it in ignorance. But which peoples of this God's world have not dwelt in such ignorance at some point in their development? Why then magnify that of the Africans? Indeed, a study of the development of the European peoples, from whom most of the peoples of the United States and Canada owe their background, show that that was also true of them.

Therefore, missions to Africa in the 1980s should be a covenant relationship in which we share with and learn from each other the richness of the gospel of Jesus Christ. Africa is no longer the jungle from which the heathens should be rescued. We have and respect our own values. We want to embrace the faith in an authentic African way.

Historical records have shown that the Christian church as we have it today is a cross-cultural development, developed through many centuries. Christianity means something different and better to us now than it did to people who lived the Christian life in, say, the 10th century. Not that the gospel has changed, but that Christian experience has expanded.

The essence and scope of the Christian message is always the same, but every new convert teaches us more of its meaning. We need therefore to be open to cross-cultural pollination of the faith. The westerner should now be prepared to learn from African Christians what it means to suffer for the faith. The thought that Christianity is the preserver of western civilization and theology needs serious rethinking if the faith should be of any meaning to humankind. As Africans the message that we are hearing from this thought is that to be a good Christian is to believe and worship as a North Atlantic Anglo-Saxon. As Africans, we are not only sharing out of this bounty but we too want to share out of our own theology and experience.

As far as theology is concerned, the western Christian thinking is one form, but only one, of articulating the faith. The African form of articulating the Divine is also important.

For a long time western forms of Christianity has been used as a means of oppression or in the least for supporting it. What sense does that make of the equality that the gospel talks about? We Africans need to liberate ourselves from this oppression which is still being perpetuated by some missionaries.

In the light of the growing Christian population on the continent, we need aid in finance and personnel without strings attached or directives as to how the donors think or want us to use them did. In 1900 the Christian population in Africa was 4 million; today it is an estimated 100 million. It has been projected that by 2000 it may rise to between 150 and 200 million. We therefore need help with church structures and to cope with this rapid population growth which is draining our resources in every respect.

Since independence it has become clear that the form of education imparted by the mission school was not such that makes for the development of the critical mind. We accepted what was offered because we were not offered alternatives but we would like now to try some alternatives. And with some degree of self-respect westerners can learn from the Africans as you support us in mission to be witnesses to the gospel of Jesus Christ, our Lord.

———————

The water does not forget its bed.

How The Spider Rescued The Antelope

It was the time of year to burn the tall dry grass that had grown on the plains. That was when hunters gathered with their dogs to catch the animals that tried to escape. Right now the fire was spreading toward the place where the gray spider lived. He saw fire everywhere! How could he escape? He scurried as fast as he could to where the antelope was.

"Please, Friend Antelope, don't leave me in this big trouble, I beg you. Carry me out of this fire. You have long legs. You can run faster than the hunters. Quickly, let's flee to the forest."

The antelope was happy to help his friend. He told the spider, "Crawl into my ear. Hold on tight."

When the fire came nearer the antelope jumped through the flames and sped into the forest with his friend, the spider, in his ear.

The spider was so grateful. "Thank you very much, my friend antelope," he said. "I will help you sometimes when you are in trouble."

Some days later the hunters came into the forest with their bows and arrows and dogs to catch animals. They hunted and hunted the whole forest until they found antelope tracks. The antelope tried to run away, but he knew the hunters and dogs were coming closer and closer. Then the antelope saw his friend the spider.

"Please, Friend Spider," he said, "can you help me today? If not, the dogs will catch me. Where can I hide?"

The spider answered. "My Friend Antelope, strength is your speed. Run. I will stay in your tracks. I will hide you."

While the antelope ran deeper into the forest, the spider stayed to work in the antelope's tracks.

After a while the hunters and their dogs came to the place where the spider had been working. They saw the antelope's tracks. The tracks were covered with spider webs.

"We might as well take the dogs back to the village," the hunters said to each other. "These are all old tracks. Look at all the spider webs."

So the hunters with their dogs went to the village. The antelope laid down deep in the forest to rest. He was very very tired from running so fast and long. His friend, the spider, had saved his life. From *African Fables* (Scottdale, Pa.: Herald Press, 1978).

An African Creed

We believe in the one High God, who out of love created the beautiful world and everything in it. God created men and women and wanted them to be happy in the world. God loves the world and every nation and tribe on earth. We have known this High God in the darkness, and now we know God in the light. God promised in the book of God's word, the Bible, that God would save the world and all the nations and tribes.

We believe that God made good God's promise by sending the son, Jesus Christ, a man in the flesh, a Jew by tribe, born poor in a little village, who left his home and was always on safari doing good, curing people by the power of God, teaching about God and humankind, showing that the meaning of religion is love. He was rejected by his people, tortured and nailed hands and feet to a cross. He died and lay buried in the grave, but the hyenas did not touch him, and on the third day, he rose from the grave. He ascended to the skies. He is the Lord.

We believe that all our sins are forgiven through him. All who have faith in him must be sorry for their sins, be baptized in the Holy Spirit of God, live the rules of love and share the bread together in love, announcing the good news to others until Jesus comes again. We are waiting for him. He is alive. He lives. This we believe. Amen.''

"The God described in the Bible is none other than the God who is already known in the framework of traditional African religiosity."

— *John Mbiti, African theologian*

31

Women's Participation In The Church

Women's organizations are a vital part of the African church, just as they are in the United States and Canada. On the chosen afternoons in rural areas, cities and villages, an on-looker can watch the African women in their brightly colored uniforms going to their weekly church meetings.

The uniform is an important part of witnessing as a Christian woman. The color of the uniform—black and red, purple and white, blue and white, black and white—indicates the church to which the woman belongs. The uniform is only one after a woman has proved herself, by her actions and service, to be worthy of wearing the uniform and representing the women of the church. Most groups have a "trial" period of six months before the ceremony is held where women put on their uniforms for the first time.

The promises made by each woman vary from church to church in the wording. All the women commit themselves to: seek God's guidance every day through prayer, study and grow in their faith, serve, and attend church regularly.

Meetings are held weekly with various activities being done each week. One week the women might have a prayer service; the next might be the week to visit people in hospitals. Time is spent doing service for the church or community. Handwork is made and sold as a means of making money, although each woman pays a certain amount each year for her dues.

District meetings are usually held by different churches each year. Women come by bus, foot, truck or bicycle from the sur-rounding areas for a weekend of singing, speeches, Bible study, dancing and music. They come with babies on back, cooking pots, food, bed rolls, clothes and anything else needed for a weekend away from home. Since the meetings are held in the dry season, sleeping, cooking and meetings are held outdoors. As many as 1,500 to 2,000 women will gather for this yearly event. It is truly a great occasion as women meet friends from other villages, share ideas about their women's organizations, compete with each other in the choir or handwork competition and praise God for God's love and care.

In meeting with women's groups throughout Africa, two

concerns kept surfacing—"How do we raise money for our groups?" and "How can we get young women involved in our meetings?" These are common problems of all women's groups throughout the world and there are no easy answers.

Service is an important aspect of African church women's programs. They help clean the church and have it ready for the Sunday services. They prepare food for the elderly and home-bound and visit with these persons. During a funeral, the women stay with the family, take care of the children and help in any way they can.

All in all women's groups in Africa are very similar to those in the United States and Canada. Women want to grow in their Christian faith. They want to serve their church. They want to learn how to keep their families healthy and comfortable.

For several years the All Africa Conference of Churches (AACC) had wanted to constitute a body that would look into the problem of African women in the church. In 1980 "Women Theologians—partners in the community of Women and Men in Church and Society" was the theme of this first concerted effort on the part of African churches for women to examine their position as practicing Christians and scholars in the African world.*

The women met together as an assembly of believers to pray, worship and glorify God. They affirmed their belief that all Christian women have a role to play in the church in ushering in the kingdom of God.

There are structures of injustice both in church and society which affect the full growth of women. Some of these are the separation of men and women in church societies. The youth are allowed to work together but as soon as they grow older they are separated. Men and women sit in different pews in some churches. The extent to which the decision making bodies of the church are themselves structures of injustice is evident by the largely marginal position of the majority of church members—women, laity and youth. Though women form a greater proportion of the congregation of churches, their activities are mainly decorative or confined to women's.work, children's and women's education, and fund raising.

This consultation represented the beginning of a series of meetings and consultations. The African woman in the church will voice what she believes in, what she wants to become, the height she wants to achieve and her relevance to the work of the church. The continued discussions will help mobilize African church women for greater awareness of their position in the church, their role as mothers and wives in the home, their responsibility to the community at large and their commitment as practicing Christians. As discussions, consultations, debates and meetings continue, women all over Africa who are members of women's groups are continuing to make their witness in the church and community.

*The consultation, organized by All Africa Conference of Churches, Department of Church, Family and Society was held in Ibadan, Nigeria, Sept. 8-13, 1980. It brought together 33 delegates from Nigeria, Madagascar, Cameroun, Sierra Leone, Zaire, South Africa, Tanzania, Uganda, Kenya, Zimbabwe and Ghana. International observers were Australia, West Germany and Switzerland.

Women of Benega, Tanzania, ready to church.

Editor's Note: Understanding a continent as vast and complicated as Africa is a difficult task. Statistics can burden down
even the most ardent searcher and what is true of one country
may or may not be true of the one next door. But, because of
the "newness" of the majority of the countries in Africa, problems are common to many of the new nations. These are the
same problems older, well-established nations have not yet
solved!

The following article gives a brief overview of the variety of
the major social and economic situations facing developing new
nations. The four short articles following this one are only examples of what some countries are doing to help solve these
problems. Programs sponsored by governments, churches and
international agencies are working in practically every country,
helping solve these tremendous social and economic problems
so that health care, food, shelter, employment and education
are available for all people.

Africa: The Overburdened Continent

by Magaga Alot

Africa's basic social and economic problems overburden it
even before its refugee crisis is taken into account. The continent which affords asylum to the largest number of refugees in
the world is also the continent least able to bear the burden.

Refugee needs—food, shelter, health care, education, employment—are high and rising. In Africa, those same needs
cannot be met for millions of the permanent residents of most
areas, let alone for the refugees.

Health facilities are severely limited. The ratio of physicians
to people is between 1 to every 5,000 persons and 1 to every
15,000 persons. In almost all the African countries, less than
half of the population have access to safe water, while malnutrition and undernourishment are widespread in as many as 80
percent of the countries of the continent.

In the field of education, a high dropout rate is the constant.
More than half of the school-age populations of the African

countries cannot go to school at all, while only three percent of the population are able to proceed to higher education. Representative adult literacy figures are as low as 10 or even 7 percent.

Housing presents yet another major problem. As urban populations in Africa grow at a rate of 6-7 percent annually, there is an immense strain on housing facilities. A large percentage of the population in the major towns and cities of Africa live in slums.

The African countries, faced with today's recognized refugee emergency, are trying their best to grapple with their problems of underdevelopment, but the refugee influx often compounds their problems and further frustrates their efforts.

For example, in cases where the number of refugees is large in relation to local populations clear strains on services and basic facilities of the African host countries have appeared.

In Somalia, relief food shipments to the refugees there have seriously affected the economy. The local population is also destitute. Some have joined refugee settlements in order to eat.

In Sudan, the refugees in Port-Sudan are overstraining health and educational facilities and disrupting local self-help housing improvement plans. In Djibouti, the demands of the refugees have added to the serious water shortages faced by the people.

In Cameroun, the large number of Chadian refugees in Kousseri, where they out number the local population by nearly 10 to one, have overstrained markets and transportation facilities, causing congestion, shortages and serious hardships for the local population.

These few examples, which could be multiplied, speak not only of the frailty of many African economies, but also of the severe blows which the refugee influxes can deal them.

Indeed, statistics giving trends of economic and social development in the world indicate that Africa generally is not only the least developed, but also the least developing continent on earth.

Out of the 34 countries in the world classified as "low income," 20 are African. Their per capita annual incomes average a mere $250 and range as low as $100 in Somalia.

Eleven of the 20 African countries classified as low income are Rwanda, Somalia, Burundi, Zaire, Lesotho, Mozambique, Tanzania, Central African Republic, Ethiopia, Kenya and Uganda. Between them, these 11 harbor 2.5 million refugees, or a quarter of the total in the world. These are the lowest of the statistical estimates. Some experts say there are as many as 16 million refugees in the world and that 6 million are in Africa. Nine of these countries, all but Lesotho and Mozambique, are part of this "Central Africa" study.

Over 90 percent of Africa's refugees live in Sub-Sahara Africa, and this is where the largest incidence and manifestation of poverty in the world are confronted. Between a third and a half of the population of Sub-Sahara Africa are known to live in absolute poverty.

Indeed, studies reveal that 69 percent of Africa's population, over 224 million people, suffer "serious poverty" with incomes of less than $115 per capita per year. A large portion of the remaining are considered as "destitute," living on the borderline of survival with incomes below $59 per capita per year.

The African countries suffer from extremely low levels of industrialization with between 60 and 90 percent of their work forces engaged in agriculture. Therefore they are highly dependent on expensive foreign manufactured imports and are now importers of basic food stuffs, bearing the brunt of constant food shortages and widespread famine on the continent.

Between 1964 and 1967, African countries imported 3.3 million metric tons of food annually, this figure rising to 5 million metric tons in the years 1972-74. During the 70s, population growth in Africa was double the pace of food production.

Africa's continual population growth had its effect not only on food supplies resulting in widespread famine, but also on employment. For every one employment opportunity created on the continent there is a population increase of six more persons. Africa today has the largest number, nearly 50 percent, of the world's unemployed or underemployed persons.

Moreover, as population grows, heavy demands are made on the land, leading to desertification, the spreading of the desert because of lack of trees and vegetables to hold it back, and other threats to the delicate ecology. In this connection it may be shocking to realize that 55 percent of Africa is already or likely to be affected by desertification.

On the whole, and as prices of industrialized countries' manufacturers galloped upward while those of developing countries' primary products moved at a snail's pace, African countries' balance of payments difficulties were aggravated.

Their balance of payments deficits exceeded 15 billion dollars in 1978. Their debts owed to public and private lenders increasing from 31.8 billion dollars to 63.5 billion dollars from 1975 to 1979. The African countries face intense pressure both in their external accounts and domestic economies.

In spite of all these problems afflicting Africa today, it is nevertheless rich in natural resources and people-power potential. Today's least developed continent could be tomorrow's most resourceful one.

From *ICARA REPORT*, published by the Secretariat of the International Conference on Assistance to Refugees. Edited for this publication.

Beggar

There he stoops all day. Wrinkled Gray-haired Senile

With his stained beard, and his pavement bowl.

Hand hopefully outstretched Entreating Entreating with his eyes

Entreating with his tongue Entreating with his hand

Yet we saunter by Eyes earthwards riveted

Sometimes a knurled stick Sometimes none Always a filthy kanzu

The tattered kanzu We have observed his sightless Deaf and dumb

We have seen him piteously hopping Hobbling and crawling

Still, we ignore the gnarled palm Still we pore over the drab pavement.

Perhaps he is blind Pitiful. Yet he misses not every proffered coin

Though the gesture is silent. Perhaps he can see? So we stalk past

So we ignore old age So we condemn bare poverty!

Tanzania Faces Famine Again

by Abdulla A. Riyami

In order to abate a new impending famine threat, Prime Minister Cleopa Msuya urged the rural people in Tanzania to increase their efforts to produce more food crops. He explained that in 1981 the harvest of the staple food crop—maize—was poor, adding that the country would not have "enough food at around March of next year." This was in 1981. In this case, Msuya also called on leaders to encourage a nationwide irrigation farming campaign and generally to stress increased food production.

During 1974-75 Tanzania had a food crisis, but at that time the country had foreign exchange reserves to import the food required to feed the nation. The situation now is different. In the future, the food crisis will come at a time when the country is short of foreign exchange reserves.

The main reasons for the country's food shortages are bad weather, droughts, too much rain and lack of post-harvest crop handling facilities including poor storage.

Tanzania is largely an agricultural country of farmers of small plots, mainly using manual and animal labor and hand tools. Large-scale farming is limited to estates engaged in coffee, tea and tobacco, while state-operated farms concentrate on wheat, rice, sugar, sisal and livestock.

In order to increase both food and cash crop production, the government welcomes establishment of large-scale farming by private investors. It said that the time had come to move away from subsistence agriculture and embark on large-scale farming through communal villages and block farms, state farms as well as private farms. It is time for farmers to discard primitive methods inherited from their grandfathers, and engage in modern farming using fertilizers and expert agricultural advice. This is the only way to increase production of cash and food crops. Under the current five-year development plan for 1981-82 to 1985-86, 20 percent of the total national investment would go to the agricultural sector.

In order for the country to become self-sufficient in food crops, the government has also taken steps to increase producers' prices. Officials note that it is Tanzania's aim to make the agricultural sector produce sufficient food to feed the population and enough cash crops and raw materials for the country's industries. Their ability to meet these goals can mean the difference between development and destitution for millions of its people.

From All Africa Press Service, Sept. 7, 1981. Edited for this publication.

Local Participation Key To Water Conservation

Malawi, an East African landlocked country with a population of just over five million persons, has developed a national strategy to deal with its needs for drinking water. Planners found that community participation is the keystone to success.

The goal, to provide everyone with a safe drinking water supply no more than one quarter mile away by 1990, has been assigned a high priority by the government. The target is feasible as clean water is already available to about 70 percent of the country's urban dwellers and to 35 percent of the rural inhabitants. Rural people make up 90 percent of the population.

Malawi's approach, developed over a 10-year period, takes into consideration the country's diverse geographical conditions and natural resource endowment, available sources of finance, suitable technologies, and the people's skills, motivation and cooperative spirit. It also includes planning for water to increase food production.

The Malawi model can be applied to other nations or geographical areas needing clean water. Malawi's land area of 45,747 square miles contains varied geographical conditions that require different types of water supply systems.

Lake Malawi, which forms half the country's eastern border, provides a ready supply for those living along its shores. Rivers and streams in the mountains above the agricultural plains can be tapped to supply the villages below through gravity systems. These will ultimately serve between 30 to 50 percent of the rural populations. In low laying areas, called *dambo*, with high water tables, shallow wells ranging down to 30 feet can serve as the chief source for 25 to 35 percent of the rural inhabitants. Another 25 to 35 percent must depend upon boreholes, deep wells fitted with hand pumps.

The gravity system has marked advantages where it is a geographical feasibility. The water is soft and thus of preferable quality. The technology is uncomplicated. Water is piped from mountain sources into settling tanks and then into villages.

Since the villages provide the pipe trenches, main costs are for the pipe. Little operating or maintenance costs are incurred by the government, as these responsibilities are assumed by persons chosen by the community and trained to keep the system in good order.

Villagers obtain their water free of charge and gain a feeling of self-confidence in their ability to participate in their country's development process through their involvement in planning, construction and maintenance.

In areas where new gravity water supply systems were installed, villagers were visibly delighted and celebrated the opening of each tap with singing and dancing. Improved health was quickly evident when a cholera epidemic hit the country. Although 20 persons in an average village without the new water systems were affected, villages with tap water reported no more than one person with the disease.

With self-help labor, gravity systems are constructed at amazingly low costs, which rarely exceeded $10 per capita, even with training costs. They are designed to last 100 years and operating costs are nil. The commitment of the government of Malawi together with the vital contributions of local people, and with some external support, make it almost certain that Malawi will meet the decade's goal of water for all by 1990.

From The Church Woman, April/May 1981. Edited for this publication.

———

—Annually, water-related diseases claim 15 million children's lives before they reach the age of five. Women too are vulnerable to water borne diseases.

Zambia Tackling Education Crisis

by Gabriel M. Nkunika

In Zambia only 22,000 students out of 143,000 who sat for the examinations in 1981 had the chance to go into their next level of schooling. The remaining 121,000 were just left in the cold with very little hope for the future. The plight of secondary education is a chronic disease in the Zambian system of education and threatens the educational policy which is commanded to provide education for all.

The shortage of secondary schools in Zambia has also affected the peace of the country. There is a high rate of juvenile delinquents in cities and big towns as dropouts roam about the streets, doing nothing apart from selling cigarettes which the government considers an illegal business. These are youngsters who are completely unprepared for life on their own. They cannot be offered jobs because they don't have basic education.

Some self-reliance efforts are being developed. Parents and chiefs of Choma district intend to build a secondary school themselves.

For those already out of school, the government, private organizations and individuals have launched training schemes to enable them to be self-reliant. In Kitwe, the city council has launched a Youth Vocational Course, training male dropouts in modern ways of farming. And when they finish, some will be absorbed into state farms where they would become supervisors over the farm laborers. The rest will go to work on their own, mostly as commercial growers. There are similar courses in other cities. A carpentry school where these dropouts go for training has also been started.

For girls, the Young Women's Christian Association at Mindolo Ecumenical Foundation in Kitwe is running a School Leavers Project. The course trains the young women in cooking, poultry, needlework and tailoring. When they finish they go to work in community development, teaching adults modern skills. And those who excel in tailoring, find employment with textile factories.

One company has a training institution which trains youth as electricians and television and radio repairers. The most competent students are taken by the company while others will find jobs with other companies.

Even as these efforts are being made to rectify the problem of secondary school shortages and the plight of dropouts, success remains debatable. Even with the best conditions, overcoming this problem requires a long-term commitment.

From All Africa Press Service, Sept. 7, 1981. Edited for this publication.

Cooking outdoors in Yombana, Sierra Leone.

Women's Work is Never Done

A day in the life of a typical rural African woman.

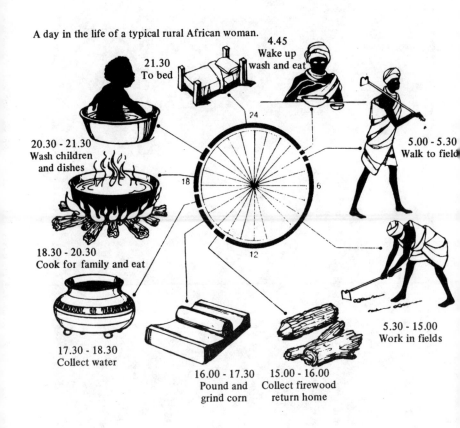

4.45
Wake up
wash and eat

21.30
To bed

5.00 - 5.30
Walk to field

20.30 - 21.30
Wash children
and dishes

18.30 - 20.30
Cook for family and eat

5.30 - 15.00
Work in fields

17.30 - 18.30
Collect water

16.00 - 17.30
Pound and
grind corn

15.00 - 16.00
Collect firewood
return home

Women in the Hunger Cycle

Birth to six months
— most babies pro-
tected by breast-feeding.
But overworked and
under-nourished
mothers mean babies
at risk.

One baby in six is born
underweight and is
vulnerable to disease
and early death.

Six months to two years
— poverty and lack of
parental education can
mean inadequate solid
foods, and unhygienic
environment — death
rate rises to 30 or 40
times as high as in
rich countries.

Inadequate diet and
heavy workload for
pregnant mothers.

Age three — possibility
of mental stunting
because of malnutrition
or because listless child
does not demand the
stimulation needed for
mental development.

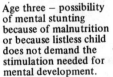

Low-paid job —
unable to afford the
right foods in the
right quantities.

Lack of energy
and poor
performance
at school.

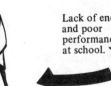

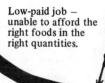

Women Refugees Face Double Shock

by Fibi Munene

Most of the women refugees who arrive in Kenya are widows with children and many of them suffer from the shock of having to look after a large family with meager support in a foreign country.

Even in the cases where the women are not widows, they have suffered. Their special needs, as women caring for large numbers of children in the family, pose unrelieved strain.

Ansela, Maria and Ruthina are married to John Lusile, a refugee from Rwanda, who has lived in Kenya since 1964. With 31 children, this is one of the largest refugee families in Nairobi. Ruthina has 10 children and is the only wife who lives with Lusile. She and her children look emaciated especially in their tattered clothes. She has recently become mentally disturbed. Her husband maintains that this is because of the hard conditions of living.

Lusile's other wives, Maria and Ansela, live alone with their children. For a long time they had to fend for themselves before they could convince the relief agencies that, despite being married to Lusile, they were in effect separately in charge as heads of their families.

True, voluntary agencies and the United Nations put forth a great effort to keep refugees out of misery, but often many refugee needs are not met sufficiently. There are many problems of psychological stress that refugees, particularly women refugees undergo. It is not difficult to see why women and children refugees in Africa suffer the most. Whenever a refugee situation separates a family, it is the woman who is left carrying the baby. The fact that a majority of Africa's women refugees are illiterate also makes it difficult for them to find employment. There is therefore a tendency for many of them to remain "on the dole," with little hope of ever becoming self-supporting.

The situation would have been somewhat relieved had refugee services in Africa paid closer attention to the special needs of women and children. They should have paid special attention to services such as family planning, maternal and child health, provision of education and employment. These enable women to lead more stable, dignified and self-sufficient lives. The absence of effective measures in these areas has resulted in some women refugees amassing debts and resorting to prostitution and crimes such as drug trafficking in order to earn a living.

It is not enough to simply try to keep refugees at survival levels. Measures should be taken which assure them of a wholesome, healthy and purposeful existence. Educational programs, training in skills for crafts and handcraft production, and aid to set up small businesses are some of the most important services that should be assured all refugee women.

The need to sensitize people about the plight of refugees—about the refugees' need to be well accepted and respected in the societies where they live—is extremely important. Many people are simply not aware that the majority of refugees in Africa are women and children who genuinely need help. Of the many points that should be driven home about refugees, this is the major one.

From *ICARA REPORT*, No. 2, Feb. 19, 1981.

FACTS ABOUT THIRD WORLD WOMEN

—Two out of three illiterate persons in the world today are female. Yet as mothers, they are the most important primary health care workers, nutritionists, and educators of the next generation.

—In developing countries, women head one-third of rural families, yet being female often means the burden of being poor. Without education, special training or skills, women live in poverty.

—During pregnancy and childbirth, more than half of the world's women have no trained help. Only 15 percent of rural people in Third World countries have access to modern health care.

—25 million women each year suffer serious illness or complications during pregnancy or in giving birth.

—75 percent of the health problems of the developing world could be prevented by better nutrition, water sanitation, and immunization. But 80 percent of their medical and health budgets are devoted to doctors, hospitals and services that serve a small proportion of the population.

Confession of Alexandria

A Confession of Faith and of Sins

The following confession was drafted and adopted by the General Committee of the All Africa Conference of Churches in February 1976. In explaining the reason for the title, Canon Burgess Carr, then general secretary, says:

In Alexandria, standing where tradition says St. Mark was martyred. . . . visiting the church in which his sacred relics are preserved. . . . walking the streets he walked and being in the marketplace where he preached; in the Western Desert where we visited two of the oldest monasteries with their Fourth Century icons painted on wood; in Old Cairo at the Church of Abu Sarga (the oldest church in Africa) built above the ancient Roman cave where the Holy Family hid with the Christ-child when they were fleeing from the wrath of King Herod. . . . we were led to realize that not only has God been ever present in Africa, but also ever active calling men and women to proclaim God's revelation through Jesus Christ.

Here in the soil of Africa was the Rock of our faith. . . . in Alexandria. . . . in the Western Desert. . . . in Old Cairo . . . . in Africa. We could hear God speaking to us, "in accents clear and still," a fresh new word. . . . relevant to the situations, the struggles and turmoil out of which we had come to Egypt. From this ROCK sprang the cool waters of renewal that would quench our thirst for identity and authenticity.

So encouraged and spurred on by St. Mark and all the other founders of the Early Church in Africa, we have tried to respond to the contemporary demand to confess our faith.

The Confession

We African Christians gathered from all parts of the continent in the General Committee of the All Africa Conference of Churches, praise God for having brought us together in Alexandria, the holy city in which tradition places the martyrdom of St. Mark, the Evangelist.

There God calls us to repentance
God grants us forgiveness,
God leads us to confess our faith with joy,
in the great community of
the Saints throughout the ages:

Maasai Woman, modern drawing by Peter Konoso, Zambia.

Primitive. Figure with bowl.
Ekiti Yoruba. Nigeria.
Photo by Jerry L. Thompson.
Courtesy of
The Metropolitan Museum of Modern Art.

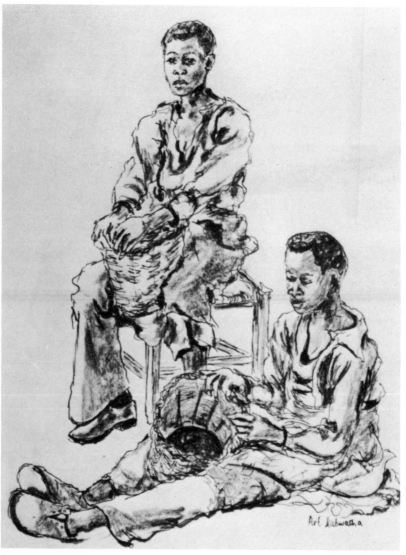

Young Men Weaving, modern drawing by Art Kabwatha, Zambia.

Primitive. Pottery-sculpture. Akan. Ghana.
The Michael C. Rockefeller Memorial Collection,
Purchase, Nelson A. Rockefeller Gift, 1967.
(1978.412.563)

Primitive. Wood with paint traces. Ceremonial Spoon. Liberia.
The Metropolitan Museum of Art, The Michael C. Rockefeller Collection,
Bequest of Nelson A. Rockefeller, 1979.

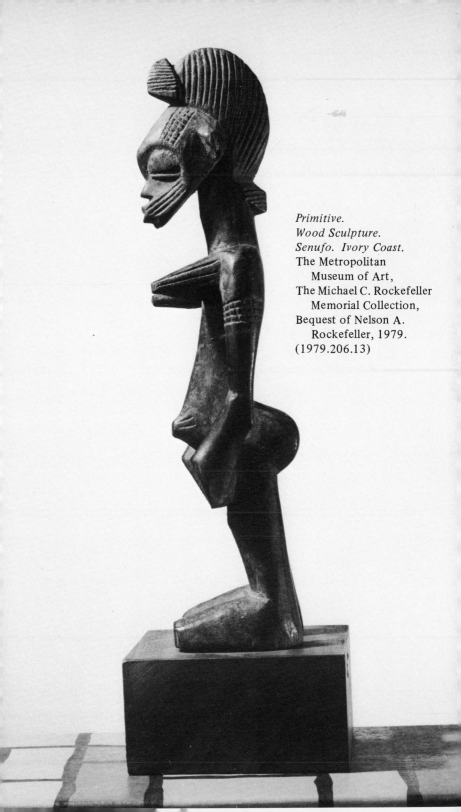

Primitive.
Wood Sculpture.
Senufo. Ivory Coast.
The Metropolitan
    Museum of Art,
The Michael C. Rockefeller
    Memorial Collection,
Bequest of Nelson A.
    Rockefeller, 1979.
(1979.206.13)

Primitive. Stone Sculpture. Ntade. Zaire. The Metropolitan
Museum of Art, The Michael C. Rockefeller Collection,
Gift of Nelson A. Rockefeller, 1968. (1978.412.573)

Primitive. Ivory Carving. Lega. Zaire.
The Metropolitan Museum of Art, The Michael C. Rockefeller Collection, Bequest of Nelson A. Rockefeller, 1979.

◄

Primitive. Woodwork-sculpture. Bamana. Mali.
The Metropolitan Museum of Art,
The Michael C. Rockefeller Collection,
Bequest of Nelson A. Rockefeller, 1979.
(1979.206.121)

Primitive. Wood, glazed and painted. Kongo style. Zaire.
The Metropolitan Museum of Art, The Michael C. Rockefeller
Collection, Gift of Nelson A. Rockefeller, 1978. (1978.412.531)

Primitive. Wood Helmet Mask. Bagam. Cameroun.
The Metropolitan Museum of Art, Bel Fund, 1971. (1971.13)

Primitive. Mask of ivory, copper, stone. Court of Benin style. Nigeria.
The Metropolitan Museum of Art, The Michael C. Rockefeller Collection,
Gift of Nelson A. Rockefeller, 1978. (1978.412.323)

Primitive. Metalwork-bronze plaque. Bini. Nigeria.
The Metropolitan Museum of Art, The Michael C. Rockefeller Collection,
Gift of Nelson A. Rockefeller, 1972. (1978.412.320)

Primitive. King figure. Bombosh. Zaire.
Courtesy of The Brooklyn Museum.

Primitive. Metalwork-bronze head. Bini. Nigeria.
The Metropolitan Museum of Art, The Michael C. Rockefeller Collection,
Bequest of Nelson A. Rockefeller, 1979. (1979.206.86)

Primitive.
Wooden Tobacco
  Container.
Chohwe. Angola.
Courtesy of The Brook-
  lyn Museum.

The Christian Community in Africa gives praise to God for God's revelation through Jesus Christ, God's Son and God's constant presence among God's people through the Holy Spirit.

As members of Christ's Church in Africa today, we have become conscious of the fact that we are inheritors of a rich tradition.

Our current concern with issues related to:

—economic justice,

—the total liberation of men and women from every form of oppression and exploitation, and peace in Africa,

—as well as our contemporary search for authentic responses to Christ our Lord over the whole of our lives have led us to a deeper understanding of the heritage delivered to us by the founders of the Early Church in North Africa.

Our commitment to the struggle for human liberation is one of the ways we confess our faith in an Incarnate God, who loved us so much that God came among us in our own human form, suffered, was crucified for our redemption and was raised for our justification. Such undeserved grace evokes a response of love and joy that we are seeking to express and to share in language, modes of spirituality, liturgical forms, patterns of mission and structures of organization that belong uniquely to our own cultural context.

This is what the founders of the Early Church in North Africa did with the Gospel brought to them by St. Mark. As a result they were able to develop a Christianity that was orthodox and catholic both in its outreach and in its cultural authenticity—and a church which throughout the ages has endured persecution and martyrdom, and still survives, with renewed strength, until our day.

It is this heritage which inspires us to confess that it is the same Incarnate Christ who is calling us to respond to Him in terms that are authentic, faithful and relevant to the men and women in Africa today. Christ's call is our present and our future.

As this future breaks into the present, Christians in Africa have every reason to be joyful. Through the continuing work of Christ, God is charting God's highway of freedom (Isa. 40:3-5) from Alexandria to the Cape of Good Hope. By witnessing to the victorious power of the cross (Romans 8) we, Christians in

Africa, are encouraged to be co-workers with all those who are called by God to participate in God's work.

The storms of history have sometimes led us astray. We have been too willing to rush off this highway into dead end paths. We have not always kept close round Christ. We have spoken against evil when it was convenient. We have often avoided suffering for the sake of others, thus refusing to follow Christ's example. (1 Pet. 2:21) We have preferred religiosity to listening to what the Holy Spirit might be whispering to us. We have struggled against colonialism and many other evils, and yet have built up again those things which we had torn down. (Gal. 2:18) We confess that we have often been too paternalistic toward others. We have often condoned exploitation and oppression by foreigners. When we have condemned these evils we have condoned the same things by our people. We have turned a blind eye to the structures of injustice in our societies, concentrating on the survival of our churches as institutions. We have been a stumbling block for too many. For these and many other sins, we are sorry and ask God to forgive us.

A full understanding of this forgiveness leaves us no choice but to continue the struggle for the full liberation of all men and women and their societies.

We accept that political liberation in Africa, and in the Middle East, is part of this liberation. But the enslaving forces and the abuse of human rights in independent Africa point to the need for a more comprehensive understanding of liberation. Liberation is therefore a continuing struggle.

"I am very grateful to have seen the growth of people working for their own nationhood, for development of their self-potential and for real meaning and growth of the church. My confidence in the church in Africa leads me to believe that they will not only survive, but will continue to grow despite the external influences on them."

—Robert G. Nelson, retired Africa Secretary Christian Church (Disciples of Christ)

"The praising of the Lord should come from the hearts of the people, echoing their souls."

Bethuel Kiplagat—
Experienced Diplomat

Bethel Kiplagat holds a key diplomatic post for his nation of Kenya. But he has already had a good deal of experience as a different kind of ambassador—for the ecumenical movement.

If the new Kenyan Ambassador in London seems vaguely familiar to some members of the congregation of the local church, it should be no surprise. His excellency Bethuel Kiplagat has been active on the world ecumenical scene for the past 20 years.

"Kip," as he's almost universally known by his friends and colleagues, holds in his mid-40s one of the key Kenyan diplomatic positions, that of ambassador in London. Yet he still finds time to keep his interest in church affairs alive, most noticeable as a commissioner of the World Council of Churches Commission on Inter-Church Aid, Refugee and World Service (CICARWS).

Lean and energetic, he has a vivacious and demonstrative way of speaking. Once warmed to a subject, he can talk for an age and has often ended up discussing with visitors and friends until the early hours of the morning. He punctuates his conversation with great sweeps of his hands, or wide-eyed expressions of wonder.

His background is humble and, to a certain extent, unexpected. Born into a Muslim family among the mixed Nandi peoples of Kenya, he has 14 brothers and sisters, all of whom astonishingly survived.

His father, who died when Kiplagat was 12, was an enterprising jack of all trades who repaired bicycles, cobbled shoes and did basic carpentry on a table in his garden. He kept his family alive and sent the boys to school—a privilege the father had not had, though he taught himself to read and write.

On forms, Bethuel Kiplagat writes that he himself was born in 1936, but he's not sure that's true. More important than such statistics were the personal relationships in a close family with two mothers. Polygamy was the rule, not the exception. These mothers are still living and Kiplagat says, "I love them both."

Kiplagat was at a local government primary school for five years. His intelligence saw him through the system on to Alliance High School and then Makerer University in Kampala, Uganda, the summit of learning in East Africa at that time.

He remembers how astonished the villagers back home were when he came one time on holiday and helped his brothers build a house. How could an educated man soil his hands with physical work!

On the way through his education, he had become a Christian (Anglican)—to the dismay of some of his relatives. New religious horizons opened for him in 1960, when he was chosen to take part in the World Christian Student Conference in Strasbourg, France.

Later, a scholarship from the World Council enabled him to travel for several months in Britain, Austria and Switzerland before he was summoned by the World Council of Churches to lead the first long term youth work camp for 10 months in Kenya.

This experience nourished a concern that he had for this country's development. He placed particular emphasis on rural areas and the role and lifestyle of nomadic peoples. He worked a lot with the tall, proud cattle herders, the Masai, from whom his father had come.

His links with the World Council of Churches strengthened as people in Geneva realized how useful his knowledge and understanding could be. He soon found himself traveling throughout Africa on the Youth Department's behalf. The year 1969 saw him on the road throughout his native continent again, this time in charge of the literature program of the World Student Federation.

Kiplagat became convinced that culture was an essential element of development; it was fatal to ignore it as some starry-eyed western technical "experts" did. Yet it was equally dangerous to try and keep it unchanged as if in aspic.

"Culture is dynamic," the ambassador says. "It shouldn't be static, but needs to evolve naturally. I don't go along with the nostalgia of anthropologists who are so concerned about preserving these wonderful primitive cultures. But, similarly, people involved in development can't just charge in without doing great harm. There has to be a dialogue between the two."

Real opportunities for shaping and fostering church action came with his appointment as associate general-secretary of the National Christian Council of Kenya (NCCK).

He held this post from 1971-78, apart from a year off coordinating an ecumenical program of reconstruction in the southern part of neighboring Sudan. "Development had to be the context of reconciliation in which the church could act as sort of a bridge," he says.

His time at the NCCK saw it's staff nearly triple to about 180 persons. Its range of activities spread into many fields. This was in part due to the vigor and diversity of the churches in Kenya and the tolerant, cooperative attitude of the government. While sometimes critical of divisions in the church, the government has been happy to see it maintain responsibility for a significant part of the country's education and health systems and development projects.

Given the fragile nature of a large section of Kenya's environment, Bethuel Kiplagat was keen to emphasize the importance of ecological considerations in development, especially in arid areas.

Repeatedly he was impressed by projects that displayed appropriate technology. He is particularly enthusiastic about local health schemes in which the vestries of churches have been converted into very simple dispensaries, a modest supply of basic medicines being available at a minimal cost.

Perhaps because of Bethuel Kiplagat's extensive international experience, knowledge of French and abundant talents, the Kenyan government asked him in 1978 if he would agree to be Ambassador to Paris. "I was really shocked. I still find it a bit of a mystery why, but probably it was more a recognition of what the churches in Kenya had been doing than of myself."

Interviewed just a few days before moving to his new post in London, he said that he felt that he would never have survived the rigors of the diplomatic job without the experiences behind him.

"Politics or diplomacy, or whatever you want to call it is simply to remove any obstacle that is in the way of free channels of communication between governments. We diplomats should be reconcilers—people of peace. We are diplomatic, but need to speak truth, as much to one's own government as to others, if things are to get done.

"Our prime goal must be the development of Kenya, of our

nation, our people.'' His energy and commitment make it likely that he will continue to play a significant role in this effort for many years to come.

From *One World,* Aug-Sept. 1981, pp. 18-19. Edited for this publication.

SHOW STOPPER

"When the congregation started singing in the middle of my sermon, and drowned me out completely, I stood there dejected, wondering what to do next. And I hoped that my illustration of the lifeless grain of rice would be understood by the people,'' said Christian Heide, Danish missionary to Liberia.

But apparently he had misjudged the reaction of the people. Heide was guest preacher at a town in rural Liberia where a special communion service was being held. It was unusual to hold a service here because it is a farm village and has no organized congregation. But the chief of the farm village had asked a nearby pastor to come and give communion. The pastor and Heide were surprised to find more than 100 people present. They had come from farm villages all around for the occasion.

It was at this service that Heide's sermon was drowned out. At a loss, he stood there while they sang. Then they stopped and looked at him expectantly, apparently eagerly attentive once more. Heide turned questioningly to the pastor for guidance. He had just reached the part where the grain of rice, showing no signs of life, had to be buried in the ground.

The pastor explained softly that the people had been so moved by his sermon that they had burst into song! "Christ was buried and stayed in the ground three days, then rose again to bring new life!'' they had sung. They had been affirming the message and were now eager to hear more.

Heide went on with his sermon. And why shouldn't he have been confused? In the far northern land from which he comes, no congregation shows such spontaneous creativity in response to their understanding of a sermon. This is the special vitality and genius of the African church.

From *The Lutheran Drumbeat,* Oct. 1981. Edited for this publication.

Africa's Independent Churches

by Odhiambo Okite

Those dramatic pictures and colorful descriptions of uniformed worshipers chanting ecstatically to the beat of African drums, dancing their winding way among gleaming skyscrapers of African cities, have almost disappeared from the pages of the world's magazines and newspapers.

But Africa's independent churches continue to exert an increasingly significant, perhaps dominate, influence in the emerging shape of African Christianity.

Not that the media—famed for short memories—have already forgotten the "independents." The churches themselves performed a disappearing act, especially in the urban centers. Now, their presence and role show in more subtle ways.

The mood of the continent has also changed markedly. It is less joyous and much less demonstrative than it used to be in the 60s and the early 70s.

This shows itself in the tempo of the continent's music, in the color and pattern of shirts and dresses the people wear, even in the slogans on the buses.

That mood may have overtaken the independents too. Huge street corner congregations have moved into municipal halls and conference centers. Large wooden crosses carried by some faithfuls everywhere have been replaced by pocket-sized ones.

On New Year's Day, 1969, one preacher at the municipal park in Kisumu on the shores of Lake Victoria told me with unquestionable confidence that by the end of the year there would be a congregation underneath every tree in the park.

I never went back to check. But a few months ago, I realized the park was completely clear of worshipers on a Sunday. I easily found the preacher, who is now an influential councilor and local political party boss.

"The movement," he said, "is 10 times stronger today. We moved into the estates once we realized people no longer called in the police because of the drumming and singing."

The movement is unquestionably stronger, richer and more

confident. Indeed much of the academic and documentable knowledge of distinctly African Christianity is based on the thinking and practices of African independent churches.

For decades now, most of the serious academic studies of African Christianity—of its emerging theology, liturgy, organizational pattern, leadership ethical philosophy and social thinking—have used the independents as primary sources of study material.

The studies have revealed two important facts. First, they show that not all independents can be regarded as Christians. There are those who deny the authority of Christian scriptures, the deity of Christ, and other fundamentals of the Christian faith.

But the studies also reveal that the vast majority of the independents saw, with remarkable clarity, areas of cultural conflict in the effort by Christians of the western world to evangelize Africa. They themselves have maintained that for several decades they have been the true spokespersons for Christ in Africa. Is history vindicating them?

The need for a temporary suspension of foreign funding and personnel—a moratorium—was first eloquently expressed by a young woman in eastern Nigeria in June 1925. When her call was not heeded, she went on to found the Cherubim and Seraphim Churches.

On Aug. 14, 1891 in Lagos, at the official founding of an "Ethiopian" church, the United Native African Church, in a resolution declaring "humble dependence upon Almighty God," expressed the opinion "that foreign agencies at work at the present moment taking into consideration climactic and other influences cannot grasp the situation" and "that a purely native African church be founded for the evangelization and amelioration of our race to be governed by Africans."

Throughout black Africa, independent churches were on the frontline of the struggle for freedom, equality and community in terms that went slightly beyond the purely secular objectives of a political party.

Not many of the independent churches were consciously rebellious against either the mission-seeded churches or the colonizing powers. Few suffered from organized official violence. The groups were devout pacifists who would have turned the other cheek more often than fight back.

That they became known as break away or rebel churches

was really in keeping with the fact of all people of excessive drive, imagination, vision and enterprise operating in a field as complicated as organized religion.

Contrary to an earlier reading of the situation, the independents have been extremely interested in theological questions. Theology ranks high on the list of causes of continuing schism in the movement. This debating is the most fertile ground for the growth of theological formulations based on authentic and genuine African needs and therefore uniquely relevant to Africa.

It is unlikely that these formulations will be set out in doctrinal treatises and catechetical statements, although scholars will write books on them and theological consultations will draw up general statements about various trends.

But the most likely and practical form that Africa's indigenous Christianity will assume will be as a functional, integrative, common base of Africa's living Christian faith and ethic. It will give African Christians a common purpose and a set of common values for personal and public life.

The independents have another real source of strength. They share several common denominators with traditional African religions, such as the firm belief in the regard for the reality of the spirit dimension and life: the "real" sacredness of human beings, the existence of spirit forces of good and evil, and the continuing participation of the spirits of certain heroic figures of the past and in the affairs of the present.

Partly because of their history of struggle with cultural conflicts, and partly because of their awareness of being God's local representative, the independents have developed the ability to tie together those delicate strings which connect the universal church and the local organization.

Independent churches provide a good launching pad for modern Africans—Africans who are not cultural hybrids always showing signs of cultural conflicts, whose faith is rooted in their own culture—Africans whose faith grows up to make a direct echo before the throne of God—Africans with integrated bodies, minds and spirits, also to move among science, culture and religion in search of solutions and meaning without guilt, dishonesty or confusion.

The independents are therefore attracting a following from men and women of diverse backgrounds who admire their capacity to develop integrated personalities able to fill roles requiring force of character. Their membership continues to grow at phenomenal rates.

From *One World*, April 1981, p. 21-22. Edited for this publication.

"I would here like to pay a tribute of gratitude to the various missionary societies who came to evangelize West Africa. I believe that this is also a fitting occasion to thank God for the lives, prayers, work and witness of so many missionaries who have lived, and sometimes died, among us. The Christian missions have so devotedly served Africa. Many of our leaders today, myself among them, are products of mission schools.

"It may be sometimes thought that, as the various churches of Africa like the countries of Africa have now become almost all independent, the need for missionary help has abated and that the evangelization of Nigeria should be solely the concern of Nigeria. This is not so. Our Lord's church is one, and God's people are one. It is the duty of all to further the work of the gospel in all nations.

"Although the role of the church may be changing with the new political and social situation in Africa, the need for help and guidance is no less. On the contrary, the church's opportunity to be of service to the people of Africa has never been greater. We are aware that there are millions in Africa who have never heard the Good News of our Lord Jesus. The church in Africa needs to be self-governing, self-supporting and self-propogating so that it may combat the errors of materialism, Mohammedanism, Communism and secularism. This is a challenge we accept. But we need your help."

—**Archbishop T. O. Olufosoye** of Nigeria, upon a visit to the United States.

"The church in every generation must be grounded in the culture of the people if it is to grow."

—*quote from John Mbiti, African theologian*

The Frog's Strange Rules About Dinner

A MONKEY and a frog often met each other on the path in the forest. The frog decided they should learn to know each other better. He would prepare a special dinner called a "Friendship meal" and ask the monkey over to eat with him. That would seal their friendship forever.

The next day the frog saw his friend the monkey and said to him, "Tomorrow I am fixing a friendship meal for you and me to 'eat friendship' together. Will you come?"

"I surely will," replied the monkey. "What time?"

"When the sun is starting to go to bed, you be there."

The monkey could hardly wait until the sun started to go down so that he could go eat with his friend the frog.

When the monkey arrived at the frog's house he saw a big feast indeed. The frog had killed a goat and two chickens and cooked a delicious meal. The monkey could hardly wait to eat.

For the first time, the frog noticed that the monkey had black hands. The frog was not used to eating food with hands like that. "How ugly!" he thought. So he said, "Before we eat, we must wash our hands white."

They went to the river together to wash and scrub their hands. The frog's hands were soon white. The monkey scrubbed and scrubbed, but his hands would not turn white. He scrubbed them with sand. He rubbed them onto a stone. He scrubbed until some of the hair and skin came off.

The frog said to him, "I've fixed a big feast for you and now you can't eat it because your hands are black. Do I have to eat my feast with somebody who has dirty hands?"

This made the monkey angry and he went home. The frog could eat the feast by himself if that's the way he felt.

After the monkey got home he planned a way to get even with the frog. He fixed a grand feast and sent the frog an invitation. When the frog arrived he found that the monkey had placed all the food on a big branch high in a tree.

The frog frowned and said to the monkey, "Friend Monkey I cannot climb a tree."

"Oh, that's all right. I'll help you," replied the monkey. So he boosted the frog up the trunk and into the tree.

The frog was terribly frightened to be up so high, but he didn't want the monkey to know it. Then the monkey said, "Whoever comes to my feast must sit up straight like I do."

The frog didn't know what to do. Finally he tried real hard to sit up straight on his hind feet like the monkey, but he lost his balance and fell kerplunk to the ground. He picked himself up, dusted himself off, and went home hungry and ashamed.

From *African Fables* (Scottdale, Pa: Herald Press, 1978), p. 33. Edited for this publication.

DID YOU KNOW THAT. . .

—*The tallest living animal is the giraffe (giraffe camelo-pardalis), which is found in the dry savannah and semi-desert areas of Africa south of the Sahara.*

—*The largest living land animal is the African bush elephant (locodonia africana africana). The average adult bull stands 10 feet, 6 inches, at the shoulder and weighs 6.5 tons.*

—*The largest seed is that of the double coconut or Coco de Mer (lodoicea seyhellareum), the single-seeded fruit of which may weigh 40 pounds. This grows only in the Seychelles Islands in the Indian Ocean.*

—*The busiest maternity hospital in the world is the Mama Yemo Hospital in Kinshash, Zaire, with 41,930 deliveries in 1976. The record "birthquake" occurred on one day in May 1976 with 175 babies born. It has 559 beds.*

—*The earliest known human structure is a rough circle of loosely piled lava blocks found in 1960 on the lowest cultural level at the Lower Paleolithic site at Olduvai Gorge in Tanzania. The structure was associated with artifacts and bones and may represent a work floor, believed to date back to around 1,750,000 B.C.*

According to the Fon tribal tradition in Benin, music came from Aziza, a god who lives in large anthills in the forest. A small creature, he holds the keys to knowledge, perfection and power, enriching certain people with techniques such as that of music.

"There are five to six million refugees in Africa. With each tomorrow their future becomes more uncertain."

Refugees and Human Rights

Today is a very critical time in the history of humankind. Each person's existence has become extremely fragile. Almost every day there are tragic pictures depicting the reality of the suffering of God's people caused by war, starvation and human injustice. The world is at a time when upheavals, turmoil and systematic violation of human rights are forcing people to flee their homelands, sometimes two or more times, to seek refuge in foreign environments. The church must focus its attention on the refugee problem which, though worldwide, bears unprecedented problems upon Africa.

A question arises as to why the church involves itself in refugee work. What are the aims and objectives of the church's ministry to refugees? Christians would like to believe that the church is involved in refugee work mainly because human rights are constantly and willfully being violated in many parts of the world today.

The mission of the church calls for the establishment of a constructive bearing on the struggle for peace, justice, reconciliation, equality and human dignity. This command also authorizes the church to protect the meek and the oppressed so that they are able to determine their destiny without unnecessary harassment. Indeed, the most precious thing that God has endowed in persons is freedom. To deny this freedom is to commit a sign of unprecedented dimensions against God for persons were created in the image of God.

The root causes of human misery epitomized in the existence of millions of refugees in the world today are human insensitivity, selfishness, egotism and reluctance to forfeit one's privileged position in society for the sake of greater justice and equality. It follows that not until such a time when human reason prevails over prejudice and intolerance shall the refugee situation in the world improve significantly.

Let's then, take a look at how and why this situation in Africa came about. There are five main reasons for the five million refugees in Africa today: the after effects of colonialism,

Teenagers gather for church.

Women work building a road.

the violation of human rights, economic disparity throughout the continent, the regime of South Africa and Namibia, and religious intolerance.

After Colonialism

Most of Africa has emerged from its colonial history in just the past 30 years. The period since independence has seen much upheaval, a natural development when newly-independent governments flex their muscles to show their strength. Colonialism, too, left behind arbitrary boundaries. Although accepted by the Organization of African Unity (OAU), these borders divide traditional tribal relationships. During the period since independence, this division has led to tribal infighting and the use of tribal differences by politicians to further their own ends.

The importation of ideologies into the continent is another cause of conflict. Most of these ideologies are based on colonial or neo-colonial ideas and not on the tradition structures of African society.

Violation of Human Rights

Violation of human rights is the second reason for the existence of today's African refugees. This heading includes a whole range of events from wars between countries to internal upheaval and suppression of dissident opinion.

Many oppressive regimes have grown up in Africa in recent years. Happily, many have disappeared too. Each one brought with it a tragic pattern of violence against either real or imagined opponents. The pattern includes torture, massacres, expropriation of property, deprivation of civil liberties and the consequent flight of citizens to seek refuge in neighboring lands.

A number of factors have been identified as responsible for violations of human rights. These include the anachronistic customs of African culture, colonialism and apartheid, insecurity among national leaders, military rule, the poverty gap, widespread and permanent use of emergency powers, and the unlimited prerogatives of security forces.

Economic Disparity

The third casual factor in the refugee-generating turmoil is the economic problem facing the continent. Life is becoming more difficult daily for people in Africa. More and more people are competing for less and less. Again, this problem stirs up the tribal situation.

Most African countries, with the exception of one or two oil producing states, are exporting raw materials at low cost and importing manufactured goods at relatively high cost. In addition, the drift from rural to urban areas means that agriculture is not developing fast enough, and urban poverty is increasing.

Apartheid

The apartheid regime in South Africa and Namibia is now the sole remaining white controlled area on the continent. The belief in white superiority and the increasingly repressive actions taken by the South African authorities against the black majority people is shown in the increasing number of refugees seeking asylum in neighboring countries. Of particular concern at this time is the flow of Namibians into Angola and especially the young people seeking to avoid conscription into the South African armed forces.

Religious Intolerance

Last, but by no means unimportant, is the religious aspect of the problem. In general terms, it is northern Islam against southern Christianity. However, the reality is much more complicated than that simple statement. Included in the problems in the prohibition of certain groups and the intolerance of some leaders to any kind of religious practice.

Solutions to the Problems

So much for the causes. What are African governments doing about the refugees in their own countries. Generally refugee groups are given asylum quickly. The OAU has said that "giving asylum is a peaceful and humanitarian act."

With rural refugees there are relatively few complications. Many countries have given land to refugee groups for agricultural development. Although the land is not always the most fertile, many refugees now are happily settled and productive.

With urban refugees the situation is much more difficult. Refugees in the cities are dealt with as individuals, not groups. Many young people flee to cities to look for schools or jobs. It is no secret that urban employment is a problem throughout Africa. Nevertheless, there are many enterprising refugees who set up small businesses with a few tools and perhaps a loan from an agency. Urban refugees provide for themselves and their families in a variety of ways.

African governments cope with emergency situations and attend to primary needs of refugees as they cross borders. They provide the initial basic needs, hospitals, schools and food. In most cases, local governments do not call on voluntary and UN agencies for assistance until they themselves can no longer cope—usually six to 12 months after the emergency. For example, it was only after one or two years that Cameroun asked for international help to care for the influx of Chadian refugees.

All in all, the African governments' assistance to refugees within their own borders is high in comparison to the help given by international organizations.

However, there is still a real need for burden-sharing. Indeed, helping the continent's five million refugees is an essential part of working to build strong Christian ties and of ensuring a better future for all of us, everywhere, Christians and non-Christians alike. For Africa's refugees have a role to play in the overall development process of our nations; and as such they should be encouraged to participate in nation building.

Refugees are human beings with hopes, desires, ambitions, capabilities and limitations and they should not be perceived as figures of incidental social phenomena.

Our efforts to assist the refugees in Africa should not simply stop at emergency assistance. These efforts should be geared in the direction of seeking durable and speedy solutions to the refugee problem through voluntary repatriation and subsequent assistance in rehabilitation and integration in countries of first or second asylum. Furthermore, the refugee problem in Africa should also be tackled at its very root well before a person is compelled to cross national frontiers into exile.

As Christians we should act in solidarity to bring moral pressure on all those who are creating refugees.

Remember that wherever you live; under whatever political, economic or social systems you now find yourself; and however remote the prospect may seem to you at this time—all people are potential refugees.

From "Refugees and Violation of Human Rights," by Christopher J. Bakwesegha and from "Refugees" by Melaku Kifle. Combined and edited for this publication.

Theological Education In Africa— For What?

by L. Nya Kariawan Taryor

One of the dilemmas that African Christians are confronted with has been described as follows:

"There is no doubt that the urgent predicament of the Church in Africa today is that of the apparent foreignness of Christianity. And this, as we have pointed out, has resulted from the erroneous notion with which evangelism was bedeviled from the start. By a miscarriage of purpose of the church as succeeded in preaching to, and in teaching Africans about, a strange God whom they have somehow come to identify as the God of the white people.

"But what has happened to the God as known to their forebears—the God who is the foundation of their traditional beliefs? This God remains still with them. And so we have left them with two gods in their hands and thus made of them people of ambivalent spiritual lives. This impedes the progress of envangelism; it also results in a very dangerous kind of polytheistic practice. Indeed, African nationalism is already calling into being a political God of Africa in contradistinction to the God of the Europeans whom a prominent politician once described as a God of oppression, a God of greed and injustice."—E. Bolaji Idowu

Christianity must never be considered a naked religion, for it always has some cultural garment. It must create new rites which are in harmony with the African mentality rather than attempt to take over and adapt ancient pagan rites, says Aylward Shorter. In addition he says:

"What really happens is that Christianity in one cultural dress encounters a non-Christian culture, and then tries to incarnate itself in the new culture. In doing this it challenges and transforms the culture. Two processes are involved. The undressing of Christianity from the foreign culture, and the dressing of Christianity in the indigenous culture. These processes, however, are simultaneous, since Christianity cannot exist without some dress or other. You cannot have culturally naked Christianity."

The purpose of the search for an indigenous Christianity in Liberia is not because we want to abandon Christocentric worship. No, we believe that the use of familiar means of expression enable Liberian worshipers to understand better and feel more deeply. So we try to make use of techniques of worship already developed in Africa consistent with the quality and purpose of Christian worship, but is the worship Liberian and African?

A people know best not the things outside of their experience, but those they already experience. This is why Christ came as a man in our likeness so that we may see and know him.

What then does this mean for our theological education? It means that the seminary must create the consciousness for self-assertion, self identity and provide means for a creative use of the African theological thinking by designing courses around these thoughts:

—African cultural elements, arts, religion and symbolism;
—African worshiping pattern and life-style;
—history and theology of the African Church;
—history and theology of the Afro-American church, African church founders and their contribution to Christianity;
—the mission of the church in Africa, all along with western church history.

Above all else, it must be reiterated that Africanization of Christianity must not only include the use of physical African cultural elements by adding a drum here and a fufu there. But must make Christianity applicable and meaningful for the African by addressing the faith to the questions arising out of Africa's long past and present and by acquiring a new urgency with the many perplexities of the present day African existence. The church cannot hope to become permanently rooted in the African soil until it begins to struggle more seriously than ever before with the problems and questions emerging from African life.

African Theology as a Theology of Liberation

A genuine African theology cannot escape the demands of helping the indigenous church to become relevant to the social, economic and political ills of Africa.

For too long, the African people have concerned themselves with the theme of indigenization of Christianity rather than radicalization of theology for liberation. But the theology of our time must involve liberation from centuries of poverty, humiliation and exploitation from within and without the continent.

A theology which fails to deal with human anguish, human suffering and degradation and simply emphasized the eschatological dimension of the Christian faith is anti-Christ and antibiblical and not a theology at all. A Christian theology which does not champion the cause of the victimized poor people is unchristian—and must be decolonized.

For us, theology of liberation is one which sees theology in its twofold dimensions—the study of God in relation to the role in human history as God became incarnate to liberate the oppressed communities. Not only the peoples of Israel, the black Americans, the Native Peoples of America and the poor whites, but to call God a liberator is to say that salvation history is a history of all persons, black and white, poor and rich. However, the emphasis here is on the poor and the oppressed within our global village.

African liberation condemns all sins, personal as well as institutional—colonialism, neo-colonialism and imperialism. Two-thirds of the world's population is struggling from poverty, hunger, starvation and violence. Many more live beneath poverty lines. Within our own country the distribution of wealth is deplorable. The people have not learned to share what they have. The untold riches we have in this country are being exploited with little or no consideration or the abuse of ecology. Lumbers are being shipped away while masses of people live in huts. The very rich and the very poor live next door to each other with no sense of guilt or Christian responsibilities for their neighbor. Hundreds and thousands are struggling day after day for survival, just to make it in the land of their own birth. The land is plagued with mass unemployment, under-employment, poor health facilities, lack of education, a poor standard of education, a poorly paid job if a job becomes available. Christ came that we have life in its fullness.

A theology which keeps silent under this kind of situation is an empty hollow superstructural theology which has no buttress, no meaning and hope for the African-Liberian people.

African theology of liberation maintains that exploitation is not only manifested in a white over black situation, but also shows itself in black over black, black over white, white over white, and red over red.

African theology of liberation condemns a country that uses its own wealth, affluence, power and money to impoverish poor nations no matter what name it takes. The property of God is love, justice, freedom and liberation. This is the central message of both the Old and New Testaments.

The African theology of liberation is also a theology reconciliation—not a cheap reconciliation but a costly one because it cost God's own son to die in that process. God did not reconcile with Pharoah who oppressed God's people by setting up a round table joint committee. No, God drowned the oppressors in the Red Sea and liberated the oppressed.

It is in this scripture that the African theology of liberation finds justification for the sensitivity to the disinherited and the wretched of the earth. Two therefore seek to provide a theological education for our people to give them a critical consciousness about their role, their role as informed and inspired by the scripture which is the task Christ offers us to discharge. A critical consciousness will enable African pastors to be able to analyze the internal and external forces around them which hamper the growth and development of the Christian message.

In this process, it is our duty as theologians to decolonize the old and ugly theology which has enslaved the mentality of our people. Unless the people are socially and politically free, the gospel will not be freedom. Jesus means freedom. It is Jesus alone who provides a perfect freedom for a people to discover themselves, to reassert themselves, and develop their selfhood, their humanity, their spirituality, their dignity and their integrity as a people of God.

From *New World Outlook*, February 1978, pp. 24-27. Edited for this publication.

Where there are two people there is double wisdom.

Editor's note: *The following article is composed of brief excerpts from a paper written on the breakdown in social morality in Africa. The paper, in its entirety, is much longer. These excerpts were chosen to address the subject of colonialism and cultural development.*

One Woman Speaks
by Eddah Gachukia

There is a common tendency to assume that when it comes to present day African society, the cause of the breakdown in social morality is very easy to identify. Quite simply we are told the cause is colonialism or the cultural conflict resulting from colonialism. Others will say the cause is western ideas and western values impinging on African traditional values. Still others will say the root cause is to be found in the economic system, more specifically western capitalism.

Admittedly there is something in all these. The only trouble here is that each of these terms is so wide-embracing or pervasive that there is a real danger that we will fail to see the tree because of the woods. As a result it will be very difficult for us to prescribe a cure appropriate for the specific ill.

. . . .In other words we must get away from the level of the African who "is more sinned against than sinning" as B.A. Ogot would put it. Until we do this, we (the Africans) will never be able to take responsibility for the development of our own African society into our hands and say, "We must put things right."

. . . .What we as Africans ought to be doing today is to ask ourselves again—what are we doing to create the Kenya we want, the Nigeria we want, the Uganda we want, the Zimbabwe we want, indeed what are we doing to create the Africa we want.

It is our belief and our conviction that the first step towards solving any of our ills is one of being honest with ourselves, by acknowledging the naked problems afflicting us, looking them straight in the face. We also have to accept that we do at times unwittingly or through sheer negligence and carelessness allow the situation to go a bit too far. We have glossed over problems. We have pointed a finger at others instead of tackling problems with the integrity and seriousness expected of us both as Christians and responsible citizens. . . .

It is also important that we remind ourselves that the world we want, the Africa we want, indeed the Kenya we want, cannot, will not, happen by chance. It will come through the cultivation of the will of God the creator, and the positive creative talent that God has endowed on humankind, created as we all are in God's own image. Any negligence on our part, any carelessness in our handling of the various responsibilities and obligations we owe unto God goes far towards the deterioration of the human condition. . . .

. . . .One is tempted to adopt the escapist stance of looking back with nostalgia at the good old days, when sociocultural harmony was the order of the day. . . .Studies carried out on African traditional societies reveal that the Euro-African encounter, including colonialism and the accompanying missionary factor, economic and cultural domination, all make the African situation unique in the way they rendered the African a mental slave.

This uniqueness derives from the fact that almost invariably, Africa's pace of development and/or backwardness today can be traced back to colonial enterprise whereby, faced with a technologically superior culture, the African's creativity and initiative, indeed the African's self-confidence was drastically squashed. Instead, a gross inferiority complex was so thoroughly ingrained in Africans that even political independence could not possibly revive originality and creative spirit. Brainwashed through "education" to believe that their cultural system and values were inferior, Africans were reduced to the level of imitator who always feels that they can borrow, without adaptation, European models to solve African problems. Examples of these educated Christianized African, who are foreigners in their own land, who unthinkingly and shamelessly copies western cultural values without discrimination or innovation, are rampant in modern African literature. . . .The lesson here is that however ideal and superior we consider the African systems were, we cannot turn the clock back. . . .The African must take stock of what is happening. . . .The African must identify the weaknesses and deliberately institute measures to overcome these weaknesses. The people themselves must take responsibility for shaping the future rather than leaving crucial areas of human development unplanned for and floating with the current.

As we have stated earlier, it is our strong conviction that despite the havoc caused by colonialism to African institutions, culture and personality, the African cannot any longer remain the innocent victim of circumstances. . . .The cliche that most of our ills are engineered from outside has become monotonous and outrightly deceptive. If we accept that as a human being the African is capable of all virtues and all vices accruing to other people, we will be able to view our problems with sincerity, rather than always trying to find a scapegoat for our ills.

We will also see with advantage, how the inevitable cultural conflict Africans have to live with, places Africans in a disadvantageous situation whereby they have to always be deciding which way of life to conform to and this can give way to or become an excuse for inconsistency. . .the "Children of Two Worlds" must reconcile the various forces confronting them and this must not be at the expense of their humanity.

From paper presented at All Africa Conference of Churches meeting.

WORLD DAY OF PRAYER SERVICES

(Prepared by students in the Pan-African Leadership Course for Women, Kitwe, Zambia)

Opening Prayer:

Oh Lord, you hear us praying here. . .
You hear our sisters praying in Africa,
in Asia, in Australia,
in the Americas and in Europe.
We are all one in prayer
We praise and honor you,
and we beg you
that we may rightly carry out your commission:
to witness and to love,
in our church and throughout the whole world.
Accept our prayers graciously,
even when they are somewhat strange.
We praise you and pray to you
Through Jesus Christ, our Lord.
Amen.

Growth in Hope:

Leader: *Jesus Christ, by his life and death, gives meaning to our present struggles. By his resurrection we have assurance of life everlasting. Our hope is built on nothing less than Jesus Christ.*

Prayer Response:

Almighty and Eternal God,
we fervently lift up our eyes to you,
searching for help and guidance
in the midst of very many problems.
Come and show us how to serve the refugees and the oppressed;
how to stand alongside those who struggle for
social justice and
for the human rights of women and young people.
Come, liberate us from captivity to confessionalism
and make us agents of reconciliation and unity.
Give us a will to love and serve you through loving
and serving others.
Keep us from insisting upon our own way.
Show us your way.
Enable us to grow in the knowledge of your truth.
Make us bearers of hope,
instruments of peace.
May we be living witnesses of that unity
which binds Divine Parent, Son and Holy Spirit into
one forgiving and redeeming God.
Amen.

Life in Africa South of the Sahara

by Ernest Loevinsohn

What would your life be like if you lived in Africa south of the Sahara Desert and were poor? Most likely you would be eking out a living with your family, farming a small plot of land.

Suppose, for example, that you lived in a village in Upper Volta, in West Africa, just south of the Sahara Desert. Your life would probably be something like this:

You live in a one-room hut built out of sun-dried bricks made of clay mixed with gravel. There would probably not be window openings, and of course a glass window is a luxury beyond your means. The furniture consists of a bed made of sticks and millet stalks, a few wooden stools, some woven mats, and a wooden chest.

Your village contains a few hundred people. The other people in the village would all seem very poor to someone from an industrialized country, but you are keenly aware that some of the villagers are much better off than you are. A number of them have bicycles and eyeglasses and send their children to primary school.

When the rainy season begins, in June or so, you and your family plant grain, probably millet and sorghum. By mid-September the rains are over. You harvest the grain beginning in late October. The millet and sorghum are mostly for you and your family to eat, but you also grow some cotton to be sold for cash.

The rains are the crucial factor in your life. If the rains are good and your crops do well, you will be able to buy some metal pots and enamel basins, or some new clothes, or some poultry. If the rains are inadequate you and your family risk starvation.

The great majority of the people in your village are illiterate. You never had any formal schooling because your parents could not afford the school fees.

In your country, less than 25 percent of children of primary school age are in school. Boys are much more likely to get a primary education than girls. For every 100 children of secondary school age in your community, fewer than four are in secondary school.

Although these ratios are low compared to the averages for some other African countries, they are indicative of the lack of educational opportunity for poor people like yourself in Sub-Saharan Africa.

The mainstay of your diet is "to," which is a porridge made from millet or sorghum. Unless there is an extreme food shortage you eat one or two meals a day, depending on how much food is available. "Dolo," a beer brewed from millet, is very popular in your village.

Although the rains are necessary for your crops, the rainy season is the worst time of the year for you and your family. It is the time when diseases are most prevalent. Stocks from last year's harvest are running out and the new crop is not yet ready for harvesting. This is the hungry season, the time when children often become sick and die.

Among the poor in your village a typical couple might have six children. They would probably have to watch two or three of their children die before the age of five. Like other poor children in the village, your own children are caught up in an interlocking pattern of malnutrition and disease. Malnutrition makes them more likely to suffer infectious diseases. The infections in turn often lead to further malnutrition.

Women in your village perform a great variety of tasks. They work in the fields, hoeing, planting, weeding and harvesting. They tend vegetable gardens during the rainy season and sell some of the vegetables in the market. They gather wild greens and care for the children, make the family's clothes, pound the grain into flour and do the cooking.

Women also gather fire wood, a task which is becoming harder as more and more trees are cut down. They spend hours bringing water home. Unfortunately the only available drinking water for your village is contaminated by Guinea worm, a parasite which can temporarily incapacitate some of its victims.

Women work particularly hard during the rainy season when people are hungry. Children need the most care during this season because they are sick so often. However, it is also the time when women must spend long hours in the fields and gardens, producing food.

Because of the poverty in your village many of the young men go off to work in richer countries such as the Ivory Coast.

They work as unskilled laborers on the plantations or in the cities. Generally they intend to return, after perhaps a year or two, to their native village, though some do not.

If there is a severe drought, whole families might leave your village, adding their number to Africa's millions of displaced persons and refugees.

Clearly the situation is Sub-Saharan Africa calls for a major effort to relieve human suffering and improve the economic prospects of the poor.

Human suffering could be greatly reduced. For example, each year large numbers of children in Africa die because of intestinal infections and other causes resulting in severe diarrhea which in turn causes fluid loss and loss of essential nutrients. Within the past 15 years, it has been discovered that a simple mixture, consisting of water, sugar and salts, can be given by mouth to replace the missing fluid and nutrients. The mixture can be administered to the patient at home by family members or by a health care worker. The mixture has reduced the death rate by nearly 90 percent among thousands of Bangladeshi refugees given the mixture. The cost of the lifesaving mixture: less than 40 cents per patient per course of treatment.

Other relief measures, including carefully directed food aid, could also save the lives of many people in Sub-Saharan Africa. Legislation is being worked on to provide more food, medicine and other relief aid to impoverished people in the region.

Of course, relief is not the whole answer. Long-run economic prospects need to be improved. Poverty in Sub-Saharan Africa is the outcome of a complex set of causes. Drought, exploitation by foreign governments and companies, misrule and corruption, tribal rivalries, poor soil conditions, war, low prices for many of the region's exports and high prices for its imports—all these factors have played a role.

The end result is that millions of people in the region lack the resources they need to produce enough for a decent life. These people find themselves caught in a web of poverty, political powerlessness, hunger and disease, with each element reinforcing the others.

A successful attack on this condition would have to involve a large number of elements, ranging from stepped up scientific research on the food crops grown by the region's poor farmers to the strengthening of local self-help organizations. Perhaps the most crucial step, however, is to put productive resources, such as tools, fertilizer, credit and seeds, into the hands of the village people. Technical skills and other such help could make a life or death difference to poor people in thousands of villages of Sub-Saharan Africa.

From Bread for the World background paper, #56, Oct. 1981. Edited for this publication.

Outdoor well.

The Christian-Muslim Dialogue in Africa

by Donald Bobb

In Africa numerous and successful attempts had been made through the years to reach converts from African traditional religion, but few efforts had been made to reach Muslims. Missionary efforts towards Muslims were often considered offensive. Christians frankly admitted that they did not know how to approach Muslims.

Fearing inevitable disputes, they preferred not to engage in painful confrontaton. Believers from these two missionary religions, each faith convinced that it holds the ultimate revelation of God, were unprepared for the demands of this religious encounter.

The command of Christ, the Word of God, to "make disciples of all nations," collides head-on with the Muslim obligation to "bring the world into Islam," into total obedience and submission to God, according to the precepts of the final and perfect Word, the Koran. Therefore, the Islam in Africa project (IAP) came into existence as a result of the need to reach out to the Muslim as expressed by delegates of the first assembly of African churches in Ibadan, Nigeria, in 1958.

The program of IAP includes:

a. Research into current trends in the Islamic world and the issue facing Muslims today;

b. The preparation of literature for Christians to help them understand Islam and how to relate and witness to their Muslim neighbors;

c. Seminars and conferences for church leaders on the Islamic faith—its history, its doctrines, its practices, its relationship to Christianity.

Much effort is expended towards the training of African experts in Islam to become area advisors and lead the churches in this education program. Attempts are being made to integrate Islam into the theological curriculum—church history, biblical studies, theology, practical ministry. For most of the countries of the "Central Africa" study, Muslim is increasingly a dominant element in the cultural context. The church cannot avoid the sociological, political, economic and theological implications of its presence and its goals.

In French-speaking Africa, where the Catholic church is quite strong, there has been some joint effort in Christian-Muslim relations between Catholics and Protestants. Participants in a seminar attended by clergy of both confessions found that they were discovering almost as much about each other as about Muslims. When Muslims joined participants for two sessions, frank discussions took place, leading to hopes that similar encounters might occur elsewhere.

In such seminars, prejudices and misconceptions that both Muslims and Christians have inherited through the centuries are discussed. The Muslims feel that Christians are polytheists who worship three Gods and are particularly indignant at Christian worship of the Son of God, for God cannot have a wife and produce a son. Moreover, they feel that Christian scriptures which originally revealed the Word of God have been corrupted by Jews and Christians and are thus inferior to the Koranic revelation which came through the prophet Muhammed. They also feel that Christians do not "pray" because for them one "prays" wherever one is, with designated postures and movements that accompany the words and mediation. "Why do Christians not pray on the street or the marketplace?" the Muslims ask.

Christians, on the other hand, have traditionally had little respect for Muhammed, which deeply hurts the Muslims. Christians have failed to recognize what he accomplished for Arabia in his time, his burning passion for the one, true God, a motivation which has turned millions of people through the centuries away from idolatry to the monotheistic faith as children of Abraham. Christians often say that Islam conquered by the sword, whereas this is generally not true. These victories have more often than not been due to political reasons. Those people who participate in the life of the Islamic community as members of the worldwide faith are given privileges and status in business and government which poses a natural pressure on all to become Muslims. This is partly because of the socio-political and economic nature of the Islamic community of believers. There have been wars, though the Muslim is taught to fight only for the cause of Allah or in self-defense. Can the Christian world, followers of the Prince of Peace, boast of not having at times erred in its use of swords and guns?

Moreover Christians accuse the Muslims of living by the law, in Old Testament fashion. It is true that their faith is regimented, by ritual prayers, the fast, required alms to the poor, the pilgrimage and enormous body of social and family laws. Judges are required to interpret and execute the Muslim law as laid down by Muhammed and the theologians and jurists who followed him. But as one Muslim put it in a seminar, when this matter came up, "Every Muslim is thoroughly aware that if he is permitted to enter Paradise, it will only be due to the grace of God." Then Christians are reminded of the words that precede almost every chapter in the Koran—"in the name of God the merciful and the forgiving."

Christians and Muslims are similar in many ways—in their beliefs in the transcendent majesty of God, in God's providence, in total submission to God's will yet responsibility for human action, in the worldwide community of believers joined together by common faith and purpose, in the sharing of God-given possessions, and in the final judgment day. Moreover, Muslims believe in the virgin birth of Jesus, in his miracles, his ascension into heaven by God and his return to earth before judgment day.

Christians differ in their concept of prophecy. In the Islamic faith, prophets, beginning with Adam and continuing through Noah, Abraham, Moses, David, Jesus and Muhammed, were mediums through whom God spoke the message of salvation. In addition in Islam, persons commit sins, especially those of infidelity, idolatry and apostasy, but they are not born in sin. Jesus, to them, did not die on the cross. God would not permit this holy man, a "spirit emanating from God," the "word of God," to die at the hands of the Jews but rather raised Jesus up into heaven. Thus, the redemption of the cross and the new life of the resurrection have no meaning to Muslims. It is difficult for Muslims to conceive of Jesus as being God, for God is so different from humans in both power and wisdom. Yet the Koran comes extremely close to proclaiming the Incarnation.

IAP uses different ways of interpreting the program. The phrase "Christian-Muslim relations" is commonly used to emphasize the encounters to be encouraged and the promotion of harmonious human relations between adherents of the two faiths. The word "dialogue" has likewise been used. Frequently misunderstood to mean concessions granted by members belonging to each faith in order to achieve a syntheses, it is intended to mean, "talking about our faiths, listening to each other in mutual sharing, each witnessing to the other." This is by far more effective in witnessing than the preaching or dogmatic affirmation of the validity of the Christian faith.

Dialogue should be a vital part of evangelization, in that Christians proclaim Christ by listening, patiently responding to sometimes fanatic or argumentative statements and quietly sharing personal experiences with Christ.

IAP seeks to develop relationships in all areas of life. One Kenyan woman has done extensive work in encouraging women together during the day in neighborhood homes for purposes of friendship and cross-religious communications. Classes are held in some Christian schools in which Christians and Muslims compare the Bible and Koran. Many families in Benin, Nigeria, Kenya and Tanzania are religiously mixed, resulting in the mutual sharing of Christian and Muslim feasts and ceremonies. Many Christian clergy are developing close relationships with local Muslim leadership.

In some places, relationships are easy, even to the point that Christians permit their daughters to marry Muslim men, although this may mean that they will become Muslims and their children will be raised as Muslims. In the majority of situations, however, where Islam is the dominant religion, pressures from Muslims may cause great tensions to the Christian community. A young person who rejects the Muslim faith to become a baptized Christian is frequently disinherited, ordered to take poison or forced to flee. Sometimes, the Christian community surrounds this new Christian. Usually the Christian community is lacking in that quality of solidarity seen in the Muslim community which guarantees a bed, food and job for the stranger and new believer.

Sometimes the Muslim families are hostile, sometimes they are sympathetic. Some young Muslim men in a Catholic secondary school in a predominantly Muslim area, when they returned to their homes to request permission from their parents to become Christians, were told, "If being a Christian can produce this change that we see so much in evidence in you, then we cannot possibly refuse your request." On the other hand, in another community, when a Muslim girl married a Christian man and became a Christian herself, she was totally ostracized from the family and told never to return home. Since the Imam, prayer leader of the Mosque, and the pastor in that community were good friends, they both visited the family, pleading with them to become reconciled to their daughter.

African Islam is different in many ways from Middle Eastern Islam. It is more tolerant. It is easier to change from one religion to another because the cultural links are not as binding. African indigenous culture is the foundation of the psychological makeup and sociological fabric, so that the Islamic faith is little more than an overlay to the traditional African religion.

Islam has a certain appeal to Africans in that it exemplifies the same solidarity as that of many African ethnic groups. They appreciate the simplicity of the faith. Very little change is required in their lives. They become members of a worldwide group. They appreciate Islam's adaptability to the cultural environment as well as the political and economic power it sometimes brings, especially its growing influence as a world body.

Several international Islamic councils and alliances attempt to coordinate Muslim activities throughout the world. Petro dollars in recent years have built mosques in Africa, trained Africans for educational and leadership positions and provided development funds. On the other hand, many Muslims, secretly if not openly, read the Bible and are open to the Christ of the Gospels. They see in him an assurance and a Savior and Lord. Their faith does not. It could be surprising to discover how many are secret believers.

IAP seeks to remove the barriers between Muslims and Christians, that God may bring the whole universe back to God and unite the world through Christ into one, "that every knee may bow and every tongue confess that Jesus is Lord."

THE ISLAM IN AFRICA PROJECT

The Islam in Africa Project (IAP) was set up in 1959 as a para-church organization with this aim:

> To keep before the churches of sub-Saharan Africa their responsibility for understanding Islam and the Muslims of their regions, in view of the church's task of interpreting faithfully in the Muslim world the gospel of Jesus Christ, and to effect the research and education necessary for this.

IAP's function was to initiate programs which would be assumed by African churches as they became aware of their responsibilities and capable of meeting them. It was to be a supportive ministry of the churches, though of necessity a distinct entity, designed to alert and to educate Christian leadership in the area of Christian witness among Muslims.

African churches organized area committees in Cameroun, Ghana, Kenya and Nigeria and invited consultants familiar with Islam to be their advisors in this new program. These earlier area committees were soon joined by similar committees formed in Sierra Leone, Benin, Ethiopia and Malawi, and a second committee in Nigeria, to permit more effective enactment of the program in the northern and southern parts of that country.

Reflections On African Community

by Richard L. Christensen

A short while after arriving in northern Botswana to serve as chaplain of Maun Secondary School, I had the sad task of delivering the funeral sermon for a student who had committed suicide. The funeral service, held at the family compound, lasted for several hours in the hot sun and was attended by almost 1,000 people. Noticing bedrolls, cots, mattresses and blankets scattered all around the grounds, I inquired about them. I received an explanation of an extraordinary custom. It is the tradition here, when news of a death comes, for friends and relatives to arrive at the bereaved family's compound bringing bedding. They stay overnight, sleeping about the compound on the ground, many staying for as long as a week after the funeral as an expression of solidarity with the family. The sense of community is strong.

A crucial question for Christians in the developed western nations is the ecclesiastical one. What is the nature of the church? After 10 years as a parish pastor in the United States, the past year and a half in southern Africa has made me examine the question from a new perspective. I share the following reflections as a North American Christian who finds himself challenged by new cultural experiences and who knows he has much to learn.

Africans have a conviction that the human experience is one that is shared, that life is life-in-community. In discussions with some of my classes in religious education, it has struck me that the students believe that the individual is subordinate to the community—an attitude one would not be likely to find in a U.S. or Canadian classroom. This sense of life-in-community can be seen clearly in the important transitions of life: birth, marriage and death. Wedding celebrations here last for days, with feasting and dancing. The funeral customs already described reveal something of the strong feeling of interdependence.

Among the Shona people in neighboring Zimbabwe, the

sahwira, the closest friend of a just-deceased person comes to comfort the bereaved family. The sahwira stays with them, tries to console them, does imitations of the deceased to remind the family of the good qualities the person had, and even makes jokes to try to cheer them. The sahwira will help the family through the time of sadness, and the family can depend on him or her to be completely trustworthy. For most Africans, all joys and sorrows are shared by the community.

Many African Christians find their traditional concept of community collaborated and enriched by the portrayal of community in both Old and New Testaments. The biblical notion of community is raised by Genesis 2 when God says, "It is not good for man (people) to be alone." When that passage is read, the North American Christian usually thinks of the nuclear family. Westerners rarely take seriously the fact that God intends the community of the covenant to be much wider.

In the Kalahari Desert, 100 miles south of the village of Maun, reside small bands of Basarwa people (commonly called Bushmen). They live as their ancestors did thousands of years ago. For the Basarwa, sharing is a fundamental way of life. They are hunters and gatherers, and whatever resources they have are always shared with the others in the band. If one of the men goes hunting alone—a rare occurrence—he takes another man's arrow with him so that the hunt is symbolically shared. And he always tells others where he is going. Any food killed or found is shared with the community. This is essential for survival because the desert is a harsh environment. But it is also an expression of a deep sense of belonging to one another.

In African church life, this solidarity is often expressed in powerful ways. In the Zion Christian Church, an independent, indigenous church, it is a common practice for the entire congregation to walk to the home of a sick member and to spend the whole night singing and praying to the beat of drums.

The community extends even beyond death. In the Maun area live some people of the Herero tribe, a group who came to Botswana as refugees from Namibia early in this century. Many Herero fear that they will not be remembered as part of their original community if they are not buried back home in Namibia with their ancestors. Africans know that they belong to each other.

This is a striking notion when compared with the individualism of western culture—a bent that often prevents people from real sharing, both emotionally and materially. This culture trait works in some ways to inhibit people from giving themselves joyfully and completely for and to others.

Koinonia, community and sharing, is a key characteristic of the redeemed people. The word comes from *koinos,* which means common or shared. The opposite is *idios,* which means private or just for oneself. For a Christian, life is no longer lived for oneself. To live for oneself is, literally idiocy. Life is life for one another. Christians belong completely to Christ; and at the same time, in him, to each other. Christians cannot separate those two "belongings."

The church cannot be a healing or redemptive community if there is no genuine living for one another. How will people know that Jesus is Lord if Christians are not willing to lay down their lives for each other? A community empowered by the Holy Spirit to give up its life for others cannot be ignored, as many churches are ignored today. Such a community can be seen as either a threat or a promise, depending on one's point of view. Or, to put it another way, when people are confronted by such a community, they are either scared or converted. This is what happens time and again in the book of Acts.

So is it possible for those with an individualistic ethos to live truly for one another, even for those outside their blood relationships? It is if they listen to the God who calls them to a full life-in-community.

African culture is no utopia. There are social problems here as anywhere. But there is in African tradition a sense of belonging to one another that often seems closer to the image of the New Testament church than what is usually experienced in the churches of the West.

What is the nature of the church? Christians need to look to the picture of the redeemed community in the New Testament, a community enlivened and empowered by the Holy Spirit, a community of people who shared their lives freely and joyfully with each other. Perhaps then Christians will see the wider implications of their lives as part of the body of Christ on earth.

From *The Christian Century,* December 1981. Edited for this publication.

83

The Argument That Has Never Ended

FIRE and WATER had an argument with each other.

Water said, "I'm the friend of people. My help is to wash the things of people. I wash their bodies, their clothes, their food and their dishes. I let people do with me whatever they wish. You Fire, aren't a good friend of people like I am."

The fire answered, "I am too a friend of people. My help to people is this: I cook their food and their drink; I keep them warm when it is cold."

The water replied, "If you are a good friend of people, why do you burn their houses and burn all their things? Sometimes you even burn the people themselves. That's very bad."

The fire replied, "You, Water, also aren't a good friend of people. Sometimes you rush so fast down the river that you upset people's boats. You make them lose all their things. Sometimes you even drown them. You are their enemy."

The fire and the water argued and argued until finally they agreed to go their own way. They still don't get along with each other even to this day. They both keep on helping and harming people.

From *African Fables, Book II* (Scottdale, Pa.: Herald Press, 1981) p. 49.

The early use of music was regulated by the African society, affecting certain social beliefs. For example, to the Ashnati people of Ghana, singing or whistling while bathing could bring about the death of a relative. Because of their lack of knowledge of scientific laws of the universe, earlier people believed that all inexplicable phenomena such as the growth of a plant, beautiful weather, storms, life and death could be explained by the presence and activity of spirits, who late became gods. Music came into being as an attempt to conciliate these deities.

Medical And Social Services in Africa

by E. A. Adeolu Adegbola

Medical work was not from the start a part of the 19th century missionary work. It was only in 1885 that the Anglicans appointed a subcommittee to examine and determine the place of medical work in the total mission of the church. And then, in the opinion of that subcommittee, medical work could be used only "when the gospel could not easily be preached by ordinary evangelists" or when the gospel had to be preached to people who were "likely to be impressed by the kindly influence of medical work."

In the following year, 1886, the German Lutheran Evangelical Missionary Society was founded in Berlin. Incidentally, the new missionary society included in its constitution that educational and medical work would be used as methods of evangelism. This decision raised an opposition against the new society among the German churches. The opposition was stiff. It was the deep conviction and resolute courage of the founders which saw them through.

Clearly it was only as a grudging concession and in the face of church opposition that the work of healing was accepted by and for 19th century missionary societies as legitimate. It sounds very strange to us as African Christians towards the end of the 20th century that Christians ever doubted the place of healing in the Christian ministry. But they did. The example of the love and compassion of our Lord Jesus Christ did not easily come to their minds. The works of mercy through healing done by the early religious monasteries were not taken as an example for them.

However, it is good that healing has ultimately been seen by missionary societies as part of the Christian mission, and that dispensaries, clinics, hospitals, leper colonies and nurses training have been organized by the churches. But for this action, the governments of African nations might not have had the foundation they now have for their national medical services. The pioneering work of churches have thus borne good fruits.

Now that church hospitals have been or are being taken over by governments in some countries, the need arises for Christians in such countries to devise new ways of Christian social action to work for healing in the community.

It is within the state-organized medical services that the church's health services now have to be administered. It will be a combination of Christian faith and medicine and prayer and pastoral care. It must include a determined onslaught against poor sanitation, malnutrition, malaria mosquitoes and other causes for disease, under the general rubric of Primary Health Care.

God Against Poverty

However, medical assault against ill-health will not be sufficient to make people whole unless the root causes of diseases are tackled. As long as we identify the causes of illness only in bacteria or in psychological states of mind or even in the lack of faith the healing would be incomplete. A large proportion of diseases in Africa can be traced back to poverty

The church has idealized poverty. We have given the impression that there is virtue in being poor. A wrong interpretation of the phrase "the poor in spirit" sometimes gives the impression that poverty is blessed. Some Christians take a vow of poverty to demonstrate the wisdom of sitting lightly on material possession. At the same time, the action also gives the impression that poverty is in itself a Christian ideal.

Suffering, too, can have positive results. To suffer without becoming bitter is a Christ-like characteristic. But this Christian emphasis has been generally used to help the economically poor to be self-satisfied with their poverty without doing anything serious to remove it. This pietistic acceptance of poverty and suffering is usually encouraged by belief in fate or predestination. Fatalistic belief is based on the acceptance of the will and determination of God.

These illustrations deal with an area of life to which our religion has not traditionally been applied. We now have to face the fact that to be relevant in Africa today, evangelism and Christian mission have to be further interpreted in terms of social transformation in the interest of social justice. Religion has to give special attention to the social ills which hinder holistic development.

The social ideals of religion and the proclamation of the

gospel towards conversion must now be applied directly to the eradication of poverty and the raising of the quality of life in rural and urban areas. It must be done not only in words but also in deeds. Preaching is not enough; social action is also called for. Doctrine must be incarnated with love and translated into better nutrition, better health care, appropriate technology and people-oriented politics. The educated who have the skills for these must be converted to become vehicles of the love of Christ.

From paper, "Holistic Evangelism for Africa Today," presented to All African Conference of Churches.

CHILDREN'S PRAYER

(Prepared by women of Africa to be used as Christians gathered for prayer March 1979)

Responsive Prayer:

Leader: *Jesus, we want to grow in knowledge.*

All: *Help us to grow in body, mind and spirit.*

Leader: *Jesus, we want to grow in faith.*

All: *We thank you for people of faith in Bible times and in our times whose lives are an example to us.*

Leader: *Jesus, we want to grow in hope.*

All: *We pray for all who are helping to bring freedom, peace and justice in our world.*

Leader: *Jesus, we want to grow in love.*

All: *Help us to love one another as you have loved us and given yourself for us. We pray for those who today are giving their lives for others.*

Martha Ahmadu: Health For Hildi

Every day except Sunday, Martha Ahmadu opens the village health post from 7 a.m. to noon, but people come to her home any time of day or night. Martha does not view this as an imposition, rather, she considers it part of her responsibility to her neighbors. She also makes home visits on newborns and on persons too sick to come to her health post.

Martha is the village health worker (VHW) in the small village of Hildi, in northeastern Nigeria. Since graduating in the first VHW class conducted under a program of primary rural health care in 1974, she has worked continuously to upgrade the health of her people in Hildi.

Martha has the reputation throughout the area served by the Rural Health Program as being one of its most dynamic and faithful health workers. Caring for women during delivery is what she enjoys most. During her three-month training course in Garkida in 1974, she learned how to perform safe home deliveries. Upon returning to Hildi she began to attend deliveries and has become a "traditional" birth attendant, averaging 12 to 20 deliveries per month.

Martha cares for the people of Hildi by giving them both curative and preventive services. She dispenses 24 medications and treatments for 30 different diseases and injuries. With each treatment, she tells a story to the patient that explains the cause, management and prevention of that illness. Story telling is the traditional teaching method among her people. From her initial training and the yearly refresher courses, Martha has learned about 45 specially prepared teaching stories. Being a good story teller herself, she now creates her own stories to match each situation.

But her skilled and effective performance at Hildi demonstrates what is at the heart of this rural health care program's phenomenal success—drawing the people themselves into leadership roles, teaching by traditional methods, and offering health care that is within the reach of everyone.

From *Messenger*, November 1981. Edited for this publication.

The Vision . . . Where Are We Going?

It goes without saying that the churches of Africa have indicated to the world their interest in and commitment to the All Africa Conference of Churches (AACC). Attendance was maximum (at the Fourth Assembly of the AACC in Nairobi in 1981), participation effective and fruitful, results and conclusions positive. The churches have spoken and demonstrated their ardent desire to build "a just, participatory and sustainable society" an exercise from which human development, liberation and reconciliation cannot be divorced. They are committed to joining hands with all of God's peace-loving children everywhere to witness the community of God which is already here!

Concerns:

The assembly clearly spelled out its concerns in five vitally important areas:

EVANGELISM AND FRONTIER MINISTRIES which should proclaim in loud clear tones "the liberating message of the Gospel of Jesus Christ." Our God liberates, and liberates the total person—God feeds the poor, heals the sick, relieves the oppressed, and upholds and heals the wounded soul. The assembly was aware of the untold suffering of God's children in Africa and recorded its solidarity with them. It urged the churches to cease to be passive onlookers, but rather to be active coworkers with God in the supreme act of total liberation on this continent, and in the world.

THE LAITY, WOMEN, YOUTH—Agents of Change: must be adequately trained. Member churches are strongly urged to identify, train and involve the agents of ministry of the church. Our faith and ministry have a theological basis which will not only arm us but also motivate us to positive action in bringing about awareness among God's people. "Come learn . . . . go teach." The right education will equip the laity, women and youth for the noble commitment of bringing about change in our society.

BUILDING A TRUE AFRICAN COMMUNITY—Authenticity is vital to our understanding of the gospel message. Someone said at the assembly "I want to think like an African, worship like an African, sing like an African and live like an African." The gospel must be presented to Africans in a way they can understand and interpret in their own thought forms and worship. In building this authentic community we shall surely not lose sight of or water down the importance of our relationship to and with the universal community. Grounded firmly in our authenticity and with the right vision we shall become partners with other communities in bringing about a just and sustainable society.

NEEDS ASSESSMENT AND PRIORITIES DETERMINATION—Every successful project must be assessed in terms of the needs of the people. A felt need needs little motivation to be implemented, that is, the right attitude makes easy the achievement of a set goal.

But even needs have to be drawn up in terms of priorities since we cannot do all things at one time. Hence AACC is asked to help member churches in assessing their needs and in setting their priorities through joint programming.

THE NEW SOCIETY—No one can prevent innovation since no one is an island. As society grows it defines and redefines its cultural life. The assembly entreated the AACC to support and fully cooperate with the churches in the task of building a new alternative society. Any change must have vision for a better life for all people of God.

In summary the assembly underscored the Christians' preoccupation with the proclamation of the gospel which requires new forms of ministry, namely:
—the active involvement of the laity;
—the joining of hands with others to work towards unity;
—the building of a community which is conscious of and which cherishes its historical values and identity;
—the establishment of a solid and firm theological foundation built out of well-planned education and reflection.

To help in the realization of these objectives the assembly has:
—given us a workable new structure;
—admonished us to undertake fruitful research, planned visits and well-coordinated programs;
—advised better management of our resources;
—strongly suggested proper planning for the next four years.

At every stage of our programs there shall be evaluation to ensure proper assessment and future planning. Through effective communications valuable information will reach our constituencies.

The task is enormous. We invite all to join hands with us to bring about that just, participatory and sustainable society we all so desire. God help us.

Until the next assembly, let us share with and pray for each other. We shall work together in "FEEDING GOD'S LAMBS BECAUSE WE LOVE GOD!" and WE SHALL NOT FORGET THE CHARGE THAT IS "FOLLOW ME!"

Photo by J. Heaton

Zaire woman.

Sources of Articles

AACC BULLETIN, published by the Information Department of the All Africa Conference of Churches, Box 14205, Nairobi, Kenya.

AFRICAN CHALLENCE, edited by Kenneth Best. Transafrica Publishers, Kenwood House, Kimathi Street, P.O. Box 42990, Nairobi, Kenya, 1975.

AFRICAN CHRISTIANITY, by Adrian Hastings. Geoffrey Chapman: London and Dublin, 1976.

AFRICAN CHRISTIAN THEOLOGY, Aylwood Shorter, Geoffrey Chapman Publisher, 1975.

AFRICAN FABLES, by Eudene Keidel, Herald Press, Scottdale, Pa., 1981.

AFRICAN FABLES, Book II, by Eudene Keidel. Herald Press, Scottdale, Pa., 1982.

ALL AFRICA PRESS SERVICE, a news and feature service of Africa Church Information Service, P.O. Box 14205, Nairobi, Kenya.

CHRISTIAN CENTURY, an ecumenical weekly. 407 S. Dearborn St., Chicago, IL 60605.

THE EPISCOPALIAN, published monthly by The Episcopalian, Inc., 1930 Chestnut St., Philadelphia, PA 19103.

ICARA REPORT, published by Secretariat of the International Conference on Assistance to Refugees in Africa, Palais des Nations, CH, 1211 Geneva 10, Switzerland.

THE INTERPRETER, published by the United Methodist Church, 601 West Riverview Avenue, Dayton, OH 45406.

INTERNATIONAL BULLETIN OF MISSIONARY RESEARCH, published quarterly by the Overseas Ministries Study Center, P.O. Box 2057, Ventnor, NJ 08406.

MESSENGER, published by the General Services Commission, Church of the Brethern General Board, 1451 Dundee Ave. Elgin, IL 60120.

NEW WORLD OUTLOOK, published monthly by the Board of Global Ministries of the United Methodist Church, Education and Cultivation Division, 475 Riverside Drive, New York, NY 10115.

ONE WORLD, published monthly by Communications Department of the World Council of Churches, 150 route de Ferney, 1211 Geneva 20, Switzerland.